The Alien's Guidebook Series

The Journal Writer

Finding Your Voice

By
Nina Munteanu

Pixl Press

The Journal Writer: Finding Your Voice

Copyright © 2013 Nina Munteanu

Cover Design and Typography: Costi Gurgu
Cover Illustration: Anne Moody
Interior Design: Nina Munteanu

Published in Canada by:

Pixl Press, an Imprint of Starfire World Syndicate

ISBN 978-0-9811636-0-4 Trade paperback (alk. paper)
ISBN 978-0-9811012-6-2 Digital

Library and Archives Canada Cataloguing in Publication

Munteanu, Nina
    The journal writer : finding your voice / by Nina Munteanu.

(The alien's guidebook series)
Co-published by: Starfire World Syndicate.
Includes bibliographical references.
Also issued in electronic format.
ISBN 978-0-9811636-0-4

    1. Diaries--Authorship. I. Title. II. Series: Alien's guidebook series

PN4390.M85 2013   808.06'692   C2013-901964-2

2

For Dad with love

Acknowledgements

I consulted the wisdom of many authorities in the areas of journal writing, diary-keeping, psychology and social networking. Most of these experts are cited in the bibliography. Others ... you know who you are; thank you! I owe a debt of gratitude to Kalin Vlasi and the *Editura Paralela 45* team for faithfully translating and publishing this series in Romania. *Multumesc!*

Praise for *The Fiction Writer: Get Published, Write Now!*:

"The Fiction Writer is at the top of the required reading list for my students...A veritable cornucopia of hands-on help for aspiring writers of any age...The quintessential guidebook for the soon-to-be-published."–**Susan H. McLemore**, Language Arts Instructor, Glynn Academy

"Nina Munteanu's The Fiction Writer is the book I wish I had 15 years ago. Writers young and old can find ways to improve their work, with the book's fun, easy to read format." —**Theresa Vinson**, Book Seller

"I'm very impressed...Nina shares the hard-won knowledge she's accumulated...I'm thoroughly enjoying the book!"—**Robert J. Sawyer**, Hugo and Nebula award-winning author of *Rollback*

"It has become my writing bible."—**Carina Burns**, author of *The Syrian Jewelry Box*

"If you are serious about your writing, The Fiction Writer: Get Published, Write Now! is as important a tool as your laptop or your pen. Do yourself a favor, and just buy it. Better still, buy the book and get yourself to one of Nina's workshops...Nina's teaching style is straight-up, fact-filled, enriching, joyful and thorough...She is honest, she is human and she wants you to succeed."—**Cathi Urbonas**, writer, Halifax, NS

"High energy writer and teacher of writing Nina Munteanu is an upbeat coach for new and published writers seeking to refresh their art." —**Lynda Williams**, author of *Okal Rel* Series.

"This book is infused with Nina's energy... Good for both published and unpublished writers, I highly recommend this book for any writer wishing to get published or push their stuff to the next level."—**Marie Bilodeau**, author of *Princess of Light*

4

Table of Contents

6

1.0 INTRODUCTION

Words are a form of action, capable of influencing change—Ingrid Bengis

There are as many reasons for writing a journal as there are people in the world: to express, to heal and clarify, to create, learn and influence, to record, to celebrate, to share with friends or the world even...and everything in-between. The journal is a way to connect—to yourself and to others—with gentleness, compassion and deeper understanding. It's a "safe home" where your deepest thoughts can reside without fear of judgment, blame or need for justification. A place where you can be just you.

From the private locked notebook to digital files to global blogs and Facebook, writers today have so many choices for expression. We are all writers and there is something out there for you.

This guidebook will help you make the right choices. I go over the tools you need to consider before you get started. I also show you the steps on how to get started and—just as important—how to keep going. I cover how to get the most out of your journal writing experience and discuss safety issues. To help, I provide you with examples and practical exercises. References appear at the end of each chapter. There's also a bibliography at the back in case you want to read more and an index to find things in here.

Enjoy, learn and, above all, have fun!

1.1 What is a Journal ...?

The words that enlighten the soul are more precious than jewels—Hazrat Inayat Khan

Most people think of a journal as a bound notebook with text, sketches and pasted-in mementos. But it can also be a binder full of memorabilia and notes, a collection of digital information on a computer, CD or flash drive, or an audiotape. The journal is essentially a "day book" according to Ron Klug (2002), a place where you record daily happenings. But it is much more than that. The journal is a tool for self-discovery, an aid to concentration and finding clarity, a "mirror for the soul", a training ground for a writer and a good friend and confidant. It is at its heart a place of learning and being.

Mary Louise Holly (1989) describes a journal as "a reconstruction of experience and, like the diary, has both objective and subjective dimensions, but unlike diaries, the writer is (or becomes) aware of the difference. The journal...is a book that someone returns to. It serves purposes beyond recording events and pouring out thoughts and feelings. Like the diary, the journal is a place to 'let it all out'. But the journal is also a place for making sense of what is out." The journal helps you assess the next step and help you find direction. I talk more about this in Chapter 5.

Some reject journaling as too self-absorbing; the truth is that most of us during some part of our lives are *too little connected to ourselves.* We keep so busy, filling our lives with activities, filling our senses with stimuli, running at full tilt.

We may be constantly communicating with others through cell phones, computers, notebooks, at school and at work. But we aren't communicating with ourselves. For that to happen we need to quiet our minds and our environment to have a meaningful self-dialogue. This is the gift that journaling brings to us. It helps us find the depth of ourselves and lead richer more truthful lives. The key is to use it to learn.

Journals help us get in touch with and process our feelings, find direction and take action that is meaningful to who we really are.

A journal can be a happy place, a place to celebrate one's explorations and achievements and self-education. It need not be the dark brooding place many people envision when they think of diaries and journals. Here's what journal writer Jennifer Moon (1999) says about her journal:

A journal is a friend that is always there and is

always a comfort. In bad moments I write, and usually end up feeling better. It reflects back at me things that I can learn about my world and myself. It represents a private space in my life, a beautiful solitude, the moments before I go to sleep just to stop and note what there is about the day or about my life at the time. I think that it has enabled me to feel deeper and more established as a person, more in control and more trusting of life. On a less introverted note, I think that it contributes to my ability to write in general, and it underlies an interest in poetry and creative writing which awaits a quieter time in my life for fulfillment.

Remember, it is just as important to record your happy, wonderful, scintillating and inspirational experiences as those dark moments.

1.2 Why Write a Journal...?

Writing has helped me heal. Writing has changed my life. Writing has saved my life—Louise DeSalvo

Writer Louise DeSalvo shared an interesting story about what expressive writing means to her. Here's what she said: "Many people I know who want to write but don't (my husband, Ernie, for example) or who want to write more than they have but say they can't find the time (my friend Marla) have told me that taking the time to write seems so, well, self-indulgent, self-involved, frivolous even. And that finding the time to write—even a diary, much less fiction or memoir or poetry—in their busy schedules is impossible. *I'll write when I have the time*, they say."

Then DeSalvo adds, "what if writing weren't such a luxury? What if writing were a simple, significant, yet necessary way to achieve spiritual, emotional, and psychic wholeness? To synthesize thought and feeling, to understand how feeling relates to events in our lives and vice versa? What if writing were as important as a basic human function and as significant to maintaining and promoting our psychic and physical wellness as, say, exercise, healthful food, pure water, clean air, rest and repose, and some soul-satisfying practice?"

Journal writing encourages engagement and reflection. It helps you deepen your self-understanding and make added sense of your life and what you believe. It can provide you with added perspective on you and the world, by giving you a greater awareness of what is happening to and around you in your daily world. Writing a journal can help you write better and help improve your skills in observing, recording and interpretation. It can also help you set goals and manage your time and priorities.

Give yourself the permission to write. Give yourself the gift of expression.

1.3 You Are a Storyteller...

I am the only one who can tell the story of my life and say what it means—Dorothy Allison

Writing is power. Writing is motion. Writing is story. From the moment you start scrawling words on paper, sketch, move paintbrush over canvas, or touch the computer keyboard, you are telling a story. Writing a journal is telling *your story*.

11

■ Your Story...

I coach writers. I am helping most of them achieve the goal of publication. But some simply want to improve their writing. It depends on who you are writing for. Sometimes you don't really know at first. In most cases, you start by writing for yourself, sometimes to gain clarity or to heal. Sometimes, that invisible "friend" you are writing to emerges into something more substantial and real. This often happens when we realize that what began as very personal in fact relates to a community and a larger audience; that what heals us might help heal others. That's when a journal might turn into a memoir or fictional allegory.

When we share our stories, when we write testimony, we are no longer allowing ourselves to be silenced or allowing others to speak for our experience. Writing to heal and making it public "is the most important emotional, psychological, artistic, and political project of our time," says DeSalvo. I agree. I am currently coaching a young woman who is writing a memoir about her traumatic childhood in an abusive family. She shares how she triumphed over many obstacles to recapture her self-esteem and make a good and happy life for herself. Sharing her journey will help others realize theirs. This is a good. An absolute good.

Writer Isabel Allende once said, "Being a witness is my mission in the world and this is what I do

12

when I tell stories."

■ My Story ...And My Dream

I started writing and drawing as soon as I could hold a pencil. Even before I could read, I wanted to become a "paperback writer" like in the old Beatles song.

It was a moment of clarity for me and despite being challenged by my stern and un-imaginative primary school teacher, who kept trying to corral me into being "normal", I wasn't going to let anyone stem my creativity and eccentric, if not wayward, approach to literature, language and writing. I was a confident, but lovable, little brat and I knew it. She and I didn't exactly get along, as a result. But I did okay anyway, and, despite her acidic commentary, Miss House begrudgingly awarded me my due A's and B's.

I wrote some fan fiction but quickly found my own creations far more interesting and less limiting. As a teenager, I wrote, directed and recorded "radio plays" with my sister. When we weren't bursting into riotous laughter, it was actually pretty good. She and I shared a bedroom in the back of the house and at bedtime we opened our doors of imagination to a cast of thousands. We fed each other wild stories of space travel, adventure and intrigue, whispering and giggling well into the dark night long after our parents were snoring in their beds. Those days scintillated with liberating originality, excitement and joy. I also enjoyed animation and drew several cartoon strips, peopled with crazy characters as I dreamt of writing graphic novels like *Green Lantern, Magnus, Robot Fighter* and *Spiderman*. My hero was science fiction author and futurist, Ray Bradbury; I vowed to write profoundly stirring tales like he did.

I had found what excites me—my passion for telling stories—and I'd inadvertently stumbled upon an important piece of the secret formula for success: 1) having discovered my passion, I decided on a goal; 2) I found and wished to emulate a "hero" who'd achieved that goal and therefore had a "case study"; 3) I applied myself to the pursuit of my goal. Oops...the third one, well...it went downhill from there...Life got in the way.

I grew up.

Well, that, and the environment intervened. In several ways. It started with my parents. Recognizing my talent and interest in the fine arts (I was pretty good in visual arts), they pushed me to get a fine arts degree in university and go into teaching or advertising. They didn't see fiction writing as a viable career or a strength of mine (I was lousy at spelling and, despite my ability to tell stories and my love for graphic novels, I didn't read books much). I can still remember my father's lecture to me about how perfect the teaching or nursing profession was for me. I wasn't enamored by either. The second blow to my author-ego came in the form of a school "interest-ability" test, meant to prepare us for our career decisions. I remember the test consisting of an IQ portion (spatial, English and math), and a psychology portion (including problem-solving and scenarios meant to tease out our affinity for a particular career). Secretly harboring my paperback novelist dream, I filled out my forms with great excitement. I still remember the deflating results, which suggested that I was best suited to be a sergeant in the army. "Writing" as a career barely made it on the graph, and scored well below "computer programmer" and "mechanic"; none of which interested me.

I got involved in the environmental movement, while quietly holding my dream of being a paperback novelist close to my heart. I got several degrees in ecology and consulted for several companies to help protect the environment. I wrote a lot in those days, although it was more about the ecology of creeks and about industrial pollution. But my passion for writing fiction continued to simmer. Magazines started publishing my articles and they became my entrance into the world of fiction. Once I began publishing fiction stories, I never looked back.

I have, to date, sold short stories to magazines in Canada and the U.S. with translations and reprints in Israel, Poland, Greece, and Romania. I've seen my short stories nominated for the *Aurora Prix Award* (Canada's premier award for writing science fiction and fantasy) and the *Foundation of Speculative Fiction Fountain Award*. I've published eight novels with nominations for the *Aurora Prix, Foreword Magazine Book of the Year*, and various *Reader's Choice* awards. In short, I'd come *home*; I'd taken a rather long detour but I had acquired some tools along the way. As Carl Jung so aptly said, "...*if you have nothing at all to create, then perhaps you create yourself.*"

1.4 What Research Shows About Expressive Writing

The creation of something new is not accomplished by the intellect but by the play instinct acting from inner necessity. The creative mind plays the objects it loves—Carl Jung

You don't have to take my word for it or that of my writing colleagues either. Psychologists, neuro-scientists and other researchers have revealed health and emotional benefits of expressive writing. The meditative action of handwriting alone has proven beneficial. Think of the poetry of laying down an intelligent pattern over a surface: the subtle "prayer" of pen to paper to the renewal of self-discovery.

Over the past 20 years, a growing body of literature has shown beneficial effects of writing about traumatic, emotional and stressful events on physical and emotional health. For instance, researchers have shown that college students writing about their deepest thoughts and feelings for only 15 minutes over 4 consecutive days experienced significant health benefits four months later (Pennebaker & Beall, 1986). I provide more guidance on "healing writing" in Chapter 4. The table below summarizes some of the long-term benefits of expressive writing.

Long-Term Benefits of Expressive Writing

Health	Social & Behavioral
Fewer stress-related visits to the doctor	Reduced absenteeism from work
Improved immune system functioning	Quicker re-employment after job loss
Reduced blood pressure	Improved working memory
Improved lung function	Improved sporting performance
Improved liver function	Higher student's grade point average
Fewer days in hospital	Altered social and linguistic behavior
Greater psychological well-being	
Reduced depressive symptoms	
Fewer post-traumatic intrusion and avoidance symptoms	

Reference: Baikie & Wilhelm, 2005

DeSalvo shares something a friend of hers confided to her: "Why is it that I always get sick *after* I finish a book, and not while I'm writing? Crazy as it sounds," she concluded, "it must be that writing keeps me healthy." Although writing can't cure us, some studies suggest that it might prolong our lives, says DeSalvo. It can help us "to accomplish that shift in perspective marked by acceptance, authenticity, depth, serenity and wisdom that is the hallmark of genuine healing."

Expressive writing produces significant benefits for people with a variety of medical problems.

Some of the major ones appear in the table below.

Medical Conditions Benefiting from Expressive Writing

Lung functioning in ASTHMA

Disease severity (improvements in joint stiffness) in
RHEUMATOID ARTHRITIS

Pain and physical health in CANCER

Immune response in HIV Infection

Hospitalisations for CYSTIC FIBROSIS

Pain intensity in women with CHRONIC PELVIC PAIN

Sleep-onset latency in POOR SLEEPERS

Post-operative course

Reference: Baikie & Wilhelm, 2005

1.5 Expressive Writing as Art

There is no must in art because art is free—Wassily Kandinsky

Art can take on many forms in a journal. You can express yourself through free-form, doodling, cartooning, collage, sketches, coloring, paintings, photographs and mixed media. On a computer-based journal you can add links to web pages and music, images and videos. You can create slideshows, movies or other multi-media presentations. Art also includes poetry, prose, puzzles, riddles, and other forms of narrative.

■ Art as Expression

In her book *Inner Journeying Through Art-Journaling* Marianne Hieb tells us that art can be used by journalers to attain personal balance, become aware of their own inner processes, resolve internal conflicts and enhance wellness. Because art is metaphoric in nature (it tells the truth obliquely through symbols, color, texture and form), it has the subtle power to express more truth than words. Doodling and other kinds of free-form art provide a rich and personal form of expression that can speak to subtle moods, feelings and thoughts.

I talk more about this form of journal expression in Chapter 3.

19

1.6 Keeping a Record

We all learn from another's stories, which is, perhaps, the greatest gift— Judith Barrington

■ Remembering What Really Happened

An important benefit to journaling is that it helps us to remember something later. Journal entries keep records for you to look back on and take action or simply reflect. By recording your thoughts and feelings as things happened, you are providing an accurate journalist's account of how things affected you *as you experienced them*. This may differ from your reflections on the occurrences and your *reactions later on*. Both are relevant. For instance, say I experienced a huge mis-understanding with my older brother, who accused me of stealing his guitar pick. My first reaction was anger and hurt at the thought that he would even think that I would steal and steal from him especially. But, then, upon later reflection, I might realize that his angry lashing out was a function of his hurt and jealousy that I wouldn't play with him. By writing and reading both entries on the same event, I gained perspective and understanding and was then able to formulate a more healthy action. By recording action (the now) and reaction (later), you maintain accuracy and gain perspective. I talk more about this in Chapter 5.

■ Record-Keeping

Maybe you experienced, discovered or saw something significant but didn't have time to think about it right then; noting it in your journal helps you recapture the moment later on so you can reflect on it more deeply, express your reactions and feelings in a more leisurely time, prioritize its importance and take action.

Journals can also be used as simple reminders for errands and tasks, to meetings we need to do and get to in the day and keep track that we did them (by using a check list). Whether this is in the form of an app on a smart phone or a page in a field-notebook is irrelevant—both forms serve the same purpose.

■ Clearing Your Mind

Mary Louise Holly (1989) tells us that "the journal offers a way to sort out the multitude of demands and interactions and to highlight the most important ones."

I'm constantly on the go, traveling to do my research or meet people. I find that during my travels, particularly, I need to keep a journal to record all the ideas that come to me. I find that if I don't have the journal to jot down my thoughts, my mind hangs on to the thought and can't do anything else (it's a little like having to go to the bathroom!). So, when I write down the cool thought I had, it clears my mind and frees me to continue observing and thinking of other things that I encounter. Later on, when I'm at my destination, I can flesh out the thought on my computer.

21

1.7 References

Baikie, Karen & Kay Wilhelm. 2005. "Emotional and physical health benefits of expressive writing." *Advances in Psychiatric Treatment*. 11: 338-346.

DeSalvo, Louise. 2000. "Writing as a Way of Healing: How Telling Our Stories Transforms Our Lives." Beacon Press, Boston. 226pp.

Hieb, Marianne. 2005. "Inner Journeying Through Art-Journaling". Jessica Kingsley Publishers, London, England. 176pp.

Holly, Mary Louise. 1989. "Writing to Grow. Keeping a personal-professional journal". Heinemann. Portsmouth, New Hampshire.

Klug, Ron. 2002. "How to Keep a Spiritual Journal: a guide to journal keeping for inner growth and personal discovery". Augsburg, Minneapolis, 4th ed.

Moon, Jennifer. 1999. "Learning Journals: A handbook for academics, students and professional development". Kogan Page. London.

Pennebaker, James. W. 1990. "Opening Up: The Healing Power of Confiding in Others". Morrow, New York, NY.

Pennebaker, James W., and Sandra Klihr Beall. 1986. "Confronting a Traumatic Event: Toward an Understanding of Inhibition and Disease". *Journal of Abnormal Psychology* 95, no. 3: 274-81.

Chapter 2: BEFORE YOU GET STARTED

*What is a diary as a rule? A document useful to the person who keeps it. Dull to the contemporary who reads it and invaluable to the student, centuries afterwards, who treasures it—*Walter Scott

2.1 Decide on Your Medium

*You need to claim the events of your life to make yourself yours —*Anne-Wilson Schaff

Before you start, it's important to decide on a few things. Making preparations will ensure that you enjoy your journey. Your journal reflects your life journey and is an extension of your personality; so its quality should relate to why you are keeping a journal. You'll want to decide on the medium you use (e.g., computer or paper), the type of journal you keep (personal, nature, travel, etc.) and where and when you want to do your journaling. Choose these carefully; they will make a difference in the success of your journey.

You can keep a paper journal (e.g., a notebook) or digital journal on computer or other mobile device or you may share on the Internet. Each method has its uses and which you choose will depend on your way of doing things. You may end up keeping several journals and their form will reflect their topics, themes and your privacy requirements. For instance you may keep 1) a daily personal password-protected diary on your laptop, 2) a notebook nature journal that you take with you every time you go out on hikes and walks, and 3) a blog you share with your friends that you update several times in a week on your mobile phone, notebook computer or tablet.

2.2 Paper-Based Journals

Talking to paper is talking to the divine. It is talking to a listener that will understand even the most difficult things. Paper is infinitely patient—Burghild Nina Holzer

Common paper-based journals include bound notebooks with different styles, notepads of all sizes, types of binding and types of paper, and looseleaf paper in a ring binder.

Paper is personal, portable and doesn't require electricity, batteries or a place with a WiFi signal. You can take it anywhere and, so long as your pen or pencil works, you are good to go. Notebooks are tactile, sensual and attractive. They are extremely flexible in their use, acting as scrapbook for memorabilia and samples, a place where you can add scraps of paper from other writing sessions, media clippings, photos and other mementos. You can sketch or write. You can create graphs. Notebook journals can be decorated— particularly their covers—wonderfully personalized and augmented easily. They are fun to share and store or display attractively.

Notebooks are the best media for freestyle

creativity.

Given the sensory attraction of notebook journals, the kind of stationary and pen or pencils you use can add to the enjoyment of journaling. For some of you, a fancy journal with a pleasing cover can enhance the experience. Investing in the right tools such as notebook and the right pen or pencil set is worth doing. Mark Twain preferred to draft on long sheets of blue paper using purple ink. And Edmund White shares that "I write in longhand, and I write in very beautiful notebooks and with very beautiful pens." William Styron preferred using number two pencils and yellow legal pads. Writer Ralph L. Wahlstrom likes the "flow of jet black India ink and the sensation of a smooth fountain pen nib on a clean page." My preference is to use a fine-line black felt pen on archaic-style lined paper in a small spiral-bound notebook (the spiral binding lets the notebook sit flat on its surface while you write).

■ Why It's Good to Handwrite Your Journal

University student Cynthia Selfe (1985) said, "I like the motion, pushing that lead across the page...filling up pages...I like flipping papers and the action of writing. It makes me feel close to what I'm saying."

The notebook journal gives you the opportunity to engage in handwriting, an art that many of us are losing. Handwriting slows us down. It is a sensual and intimate way for us to express ourselves. I love my handwriting, especially when I am using my favorite pen (my handwriting changes depending on the pen), a fine felt marker—usually black. When you use a pen or pencil to express yourself in a journal you have more ways to express your creativity. Think of the subtleties of handwriting alone: changing the quality and intensity of strokes; designing your script, using colors, symbols, arrows or lines, using spaces creatively, combining with drawing and sketches. In combination with the paper (which could be lined, textured, colored graphed, etc.), your handwritten expression varies as

your many thoughts and moods.

The very act of handwriting focuses you. Writing your words by hand connects you more tangibly to what you're writing through the physical connection of pen to paper. Handwriting is methodical yet creatively unique and in the 'here and now' of creation. For instance, my handwriting varies with my tools (e.g., paper and pen or pencil), the lighting, where and when I'm writing, my mood, etc. I feel the best when I'm writing in a beautifully lined journal with a black felt pen under the shade of a tree to the soft trill of songbirds.

Researchers have proven that just picking up a pencil and paper to write out your ideas improves your ability to think, process information and solve problems. The actual act of writing out the letters takes a little more work in your brain than just typing them on a keyboard, and that extra effort keeps your mind sharp. Researchers have also shown that writing something out by hand improves your ability to remember it. Handwriting improves memory, increases focus, and the ability to see relationships.

Handwriting fuses physical and intellectual processes. Nelson Algren (in Plimpton, 1958) wrote, "I always think of writing as a physical thing." Hemmingway felt that his fingers did much of his thinking for him.

According to Dr. Daniel Chandler (1987, 1992), when you write by hand you are more likely to discover what you want to say. When you write on a computer, you write "cleanly" by editing as you go along and deleting words (along with your first thoughts). In handwriting, everything re-mains, including the words you crossed out. "Handwriting, both product and process," says Chandler, "is important...in relation to [your] sense of self." He describes how the resistance of materials in handwriting increases the sense of self in the act of creating something. There is a stamp of ownership in the handwritten words that enhances a sense of "personal experience."

I know this is true in my own writing experience. This is why, although I do much of my drafting of novel, article and short story on the computer, I find that some of my greatest creative moments come to me through the notebook, which I always keep with me. Writing in my own hand is private and resonates with informality and spontaneity (in contrast to the fixed, formal look and public nature of print). Handwriting in a notebook is, therefore, a very supportive medium of discovery and the initial expression of ideas.

"I am certainly no calligrapher," says Wendell Berry (1990), "but my handwritten pages have a homemade, handmade look to them that both pleases me in itself and suggests the possibility of ready correction." John O'Neill (1982) calls handwriting "bodily art." He suggested that "the writer's fingers

28

and the page are a working ensemble, and alternation of intelligible space and spatialized intelligence."

Berry (1990) goes on to say this: "Language is the most intimately physical of all the artistic means. We have it palpably in our mouths; it is our *langue*, our tongue. Writing it, we shape it with our hands. Reading aloud what we have written—as we do, if we are writing carefully—our language passes in at the eyes, out at the mouth, in at the ears the words are immersed and steeped in the senses of the body before they make sense in the mind. *They cannot make sense in the mind until they have made sense in the body.* Does shaping one's words with one's own hand impart character and quality to them, as does speaking them with one's own tongue to the satisfaction of one's own ear?...I believe that it does."

■ Disadvantages of Paper Journals

Bound notebooks aren't as amenable to search and organization (or reorganization) as computer-based journals or loose-leaf binders. However, you can index them by numbering the pages and using tabs. If you leave a few beginning pages blank, you can put in a table of contents after you've made a number of entries. Loose-leaf binders can be reordered and added to. But material can be more easily lost too.

Notebooks, while being less flexible, have a more permanent and secure feel to them.

A paper-based journal can be found by fellow students, colleagues, friends or family members more easily than a computer-based journal. More effort is required to keep a notebook journal safe from prying eyes yet accessible for entries. I talk more about keeping your journal safe in Chapter 6.

2.3 Computer-Based Journals

The good news about computers is that they do what you tell them to do; the bad news is that they do what you tell them to do — Ted Nelson

A computer-based journal can also be portable. Media such as small laptops, notebook computers (I have one of these) or tablets provide a fairly small and light medium to record. You can also use some mobile phones and smart devices (e.g., iPhone) to record your journal.

Advantages of digital-based journals include that:

- You can easily organize and search them (it's easy to find anything you wrote)

- they are easy to use and edit, re-order and rewrite (that they are easy to change may not be an advantage)

- you can add to them and in no special order by text download via flash-drive or email from entries in the field

- you can include multimedia like video, pictures, drawings, links to other sources and sharing

- They are secure (no need to hide anything; just remember your password)

Several journal software packages are available that provide attractive templates for journal-keeping. For instance, "My Journal", "The Journal", "Life Journal" are all good template packages for Windows-based and Mac computers. "Memoires" is an excellent and attractive package for Apple computers.

Journal-keeping software packages include most Windows and Mac-based versions. They all include secure encryption through passwords (and more, if you wish). Most platforms are easy to use with good editing and search features. Some have additional creative writing modules and include Twitter portals, website or blog uploads. Costs vary from free to $50.00 for software package download. Customer service may vary, although basic support is available on all the packages I checked. Most packages have a free trial download for you to check out their features before you decide to purchase. Computer-based journals can be kept safe through password encryption, so even if someone got into your computer, it would be hard for them to break into your private file. I talk more about safety measures in Chapter 6.

■ "My Journal"

"My Journal" by Boise Software is a windows-based journal package. "My Journal" lets you keep track of your daily activities through calendar and time management software. You can keep your friends up to date with the Twitter portal, edit blogs on your Blogspot account, upload select journal entries to your own website, and use the creative writing module. "My Journal" also has spell check optimization, adds time stamp toolbar button to journal editor, changes scapegoat document to .rtf, and makes help more substantive. Its developer, Mike Snow, assures me that the software, once downloaded, runs on your computer (no need for the Internet) and includes photo-editing tools (e.g., crop, rotate, resize, etc.). My Journal costs US $19.95 with a free 30-day trial download.

■ "The Journal"

DavidRM Software's "The Journal" runs on most Windows-based computers. Although currently there is no Mac-specific version, "The Journal" can be run on a Mac if you use a Windows emulator, such as "Virtual PC" or (for the IntelMacs) "Parallels". "The Journal" includes standard word-processing features, multi-media storage, a good search engine (by topic, entry, tag word, etc.), organization with nested entries, printing for binding, calendar features for task and event management, and web-posting. They also offer a newsletter that includes articles on journaling and updates. The journal is password protected and you can further set the level of security. Customer service is good and includes a FAQ section, knowledge database search section and contact email. The software also includes a built-in help section and a long list of writing and journaling prompts. It comes with several skins/themes and some simple templates for daily calendar-based entries and "notebook" freestyle entries. The software package costs US $49.95. A 45-day free trial is available.

■ "Life Journal"

"Life Journal" by Chronicles Software Company is an award winning personal journal software for Windows-based users. There are ways to use "Life Journal" on a Mac, but they aren't very friendly. Simple yet sophisticated, this journal software, created by long-time journal writers with add-ons by internationally known journal writing experts is recommended by the International Association for Journal Writing. It has very similar features to the two previous software packages.

The software includes a tracking feature (with up to 10 scales you can track your health, energy, etc.); customizing for skins/themes, prompts and quotes; search and tagging feature, "Life Journal" comes with an extensive support program of articles, quotes, interviews with journalists, and other resource materials. They offer good customer service, including a help center where you can search their knowledge base articles, browse public discussions, or create a new discussion if you're having trouble. "Life Journal" sells for US $44.95. A free trial version is available.

■ "Memoires"

"Memoires" is a journaling software package specifically de-signed for Mac computers. As with the above packages for Windows-based computers, this software allows you to encrypt your journal with a password, create multiple entries per day, change fonts and colors, insert pictures and draw sketches, browse or quickly search entries through the calendar feature or view all entries in one list. The Quick Drawing feature of "Memoires" lets you free-draw and doodle as well as create more sophisticated images. They feature full screen editing, printing options, spelling and grammar corrections and auto-saving. The basic package sells for US $29.95. A free trial is available. One blogger mentioned how she used her iPhone to make her initial entry, then emailed it to her computer and cut/pasted it along with iPhotos to her "Memoires" when she was home. Since her entry, many journal apps have been created for mobile devices like iPhone, iPod Touch, Blackberries and Androids. Check out my section on these below.

■ Disadvantages of Computer-Based Journals

Computer based journals are not as intimate or sensual as notebook journals. They are also too easy to edit and change, leaving no trace of your changes. In a pen and paper scenario, the evolution of your entries is there, open, transparent for you to see later. When you delete something you've written on the computer, it's usually gone for good. Some journalists keep older versions in files on their computer or backup paper files. But this can be tedious and involves paper again.

Wendel Berry writes, "In using computers, writers are flirting with a radical separation of mind and body, the elimination of the work of the body from the work of the mind. The text on the computer screen, and the computer printout too, has a sterile, untouched, factory made look...the body does not work like that. The body characterizes everything it touches. What it makes it traces over with the marks of its pulses and breathings, its excitements, hesitations, flaws and mistakes...and to those who love and honor the life of the body in this world, these marks are precious things, necessities of life."

2.4 Mobile-Devices

Thus the telephone, by bringing music and ministers into every house, will empty the concert halls and the churches—New York times, 1876

Most people now have some kind of mobile device for exchanging communication and data: a cell phone or smart phone, notepad or tablet. I recently purchased an iPhone recently. The first thing I did was check out the awesome apps available to me.

For instance, these journaling apps are available for iPhone users:

- **iDo Notepad:** one of the best free-download diary/journal apps. Not as elegant in design as paid apps in this genre, but features, among other things, the ability to password protect. You can change font styles and sizes, use it for other forms of writing like note-taking, shopping lists, and idea mining. Writing categories can be assigned an icon for easier navigation.

- **My Wonderful Days Life:** described as a very Zen-like and simple journal app, it is a great place to house your memories. Just launch the app, tap on a day in the monthly calendar then the + button in the menu bar and start typing. This one is also password protected. You can add photos, mark favorites and attach stickers and "emotion" indicators. You can index your entries with assigned markings and the app includes a search function.

- **iDone This:** this app provides a simple way to jot down what you accomplish from day to day. Daily entries can be written both in your *iDoneThis* web account and in the iPhone version. This is a simple text-based application, good for any type of journaling or note-taking. You can even add entries to future dates and get it to send you a reminder to add an entry.

- **Pad & Quill:** This is not a free app. Its retro old-school notebook design and font style is very appealing. As with similar mobile journal apps, Pad & Quill syncs your entries to all your iDevices and includes 10 cool cover to choose from.

- **Loccit:** This app lets you connect with all your favorite social networking sites; your musings and photos can upload automatically into Loccit, keeping a running journal of your thoughts and events as they happen.

- **Path:** Like Loccit, this "smart journal" keeps an ongoing record of your life via photos, music, text and more. Path also lets you share on Twitter, Foursquare and Facebook. It lets you connect with friends and Path can automatically publish stories about your life as you go about your day-to-day routine.

- **Momento:** This app works for iPhone and iPod Touch, featuring beautiful clean-line interfaces. It seamlessly integrates with several social networks. It relies on tagging to share your journal and daily activities with friends via multiple social media platforms. You can tag places you visit, favorite memories, and people you meet, among other things.

- **iJournal:** this app lets you upload your content into your digital, mobile journal. The look and feel of this app can be customized for font, color. You can organize your entries, keep multiple journals and password-protect your journal.

- **meDaily:** this app incorporates various forms of multimedia into the mobile documentation of your life. Media include music, photos, text, links, etc. The app is fully integrated with maps for tracking memories by location and posts entries to Facebook and Twitter.

Similar apps for other mobile devices like

Android and Blackberries are available (e.g., *Penzu*) and continually evolving. Just do the research.

2.5 Decide on the Kind of Journal

Better to lose count while naming your blessings than to lose your blessings to counting your troubles—Maltbie D. Babcock

You have so many choices in keeping a journal. A journal may be a daily personal expression like in a diary, themed like a nature journal (see example below) or as in a memoir around a particular issue or topic important in your life. The type and style of journal you keep should relate to you as a person and why you want to journal. You're more likely to make entries in a journal that follows your interests and something important to you at the time.

You can keep several journals, each with a particular theme or role in recording your life and interests. If you choose to keep more than one journal, just make sure that you aren't overly ambitious and over-extend yourself. You may be overwhelmed and run the risk of losing interest in any of them.

There are as many kinds of journals as there are people with unique interests and expressions. Even the journals of the same person

will differ according to the time that person is keeping their journal.

Journals fall under two major categories: 1) general/personal and 2) themed.

■ General/Personal Journals (the Diary)

General personal journals that record your daily life give you the chance to share anything about the day that you thought worthy of expression and later reflection. Because this kind of journal is not restricted to a particular interest or issue, it gives you the chance to discover what is in fact important to you. Through truthful recording and sharing of your feelings, the self-analysis that follows can often help you discern between what you *think* is important and what you *feel*—and in fact—what is important.

Honest journaling of this kind helps you look more closely at what's touching you and where you need to make adjustments. By discovering what really touches and motivates you, you can identify unresolved emotions and what you need to do to resolve them.

General/Personal journals are valuable tools for assessing the next step. They often provide you with clear direction to act. The key is to be open and honest in sharing your feelings that result from events and issues and

39

relationships you experience.

For instance, if you find that you are experiencing sadness, then investigate what would bring you joy. Most cases of sadness and anger involve lack of connection and some kind of miscommunication.

The diary-journal is like a 'check in' place that leads to action. "You need to keep two dialogues running," says counselor Margaret Ross of Calm Waters Counselling, New Westminster B.C., "a dialogue with yourself and a dialogue with the other (your environment)... Journal writing gives you the space to freely dialogue with yourself."

Personal journals can take on many forms and comprise of many things. There is no rule for this. You might prefer to just write in your journal. You can also add mementos, news clippings, photos and art. In fact, using art as your main form of expression is also an option for a daily diary.

—Art-Journaling as Daily Expression

Keeping an art-only journal, which some call a scrapbook (but is so much more), can be a fulfilling form of expression for you. This would be particularly appealing if you are intuitive, express yourself artistically and enjoy using metaphor.

An art-journal is just that: a journal in which you express yourself and reactions to the day through art; all kinds of art: sketches, watercolors, photographs, abstract form and design, doodles, scrap-art, video, sound, music, poetry, and prose.

I discuss this form of journaling more in Chapter 3.

■ Themed Journals

As with diary-journals, you record your observations and reflections in themed journals. The only difference is that your observations are related to the theme you've chosen. Examples of themed journals include gratitude journal, spiritual journal, trip journal (e.g., a vacation or work trip), event/personal interest journal (e.g., about a significant event or people in the news, or community), child-raising journal, ideas journal, nature journal, transition journal, and grief or trauma journal (usually focused on a particular event of significant consequence).

—Gratitude Journals

In this journal you record all the things— events, happenings, people, etc.—that you are grateful for each day, week or month. You would note the people, animals, and things that really matter to you. This is an upbeat journal that highlights the wonderful things in your life. This journal is a valuable resource for inspiration and a source of joy. It is a bracing reminder of the things you live for. Reviewing your entries, particularly when you are blue or need a pick-me-up, can be very rewarding. There are so many things for which you can be grateful: the air you breathe, the food you eat, your parents, friends, and community, your brain, your legs and hands. In *The Magic*, Rhonda Byrne, author of *The Secret*, describes a formula easily followed to achieve and record daily gratitude. And it involves a form of journal writing.

—Spiritual Journals

The spiritual journal, like a gratitude journal, focuses on finding meaning in our lives. If you're a Christian, your entries may be a response to what you're reading in the Bible or other Christian authors as you personalize it by integrating it in your life. Entries bring you closer to yourself, to identifying and understanding that part of you. Once you've responded on paper then you're able to take that into the world and live out the response in your everyday life. Take the time to make those conclusions and decisions about values.

—Trip or Vacation Journal

A trip journal may be created for a vacation or a business trip to a different place. It may be an ongoing journal you keep for whenever you go to a different place from home like a summer cottage or a friend or relative's place.

—Event/Personal Interest Journal

An event/personal interest journal can relate to anything you wish to record that is important or of interest to you. It could involve something in the news or your community that has affected you. It could be related to something or someone in the past, present or ongoing.

For instance, you may be an avid environmentalist and interested in your community's conservation and recycling program. You may wish to keep records of all the happenings, both in the news and among your community inter-actions (e.g., letters, blogs, media clippings) in your journal. As another example, you may have a special interest in a celebrity, say an actor or a show, and wish to record events, happenings, and your feelings in a journal. Your journal may include media clippings, pictures, your own drawings, poetry and other text.

—Child-Raising Journal

When my son was born, I felt compelled to record everything about his daily life as he developed and changed and grew. I shared stories about his cute antics, the funny things he did or got into, his unique vocalizations and playing and his little "tragedies". I took a bazillion pictures and included them. I even included a Kevin-dictionary of terms (e.g., ba-ba-ba-ba = look over there!)

—Ideas Journal

In this journal you record all the ideas and inspirations that fly into your mind. This mobile journal that you should keep on you at all times would serve as a repository for ideas and premises from which you may draw inspiration and develop further into projects. An idea journal is handy for almost anyone who thinks and has an imagination. They work great for writing, for business, for play, and for inventions.

I keep an idea journal with me at all times for my fiction and article writing. In it, I record anything from a curious object or person I've glimpsed to a plot idea that came to me while I was driving. Such a journal should be small, compact, durable and preferably come with a pen or pencil attached to it. If you carry a Tablet or smart phone you can record your ideas on it and then send to your computer via email or download.

—Dream Journal

Keeping a dream journal is a popular form of journaling, bridging the subconscious with the conscious mind. According to psychologists, dreams can provide insight from the sub-conscious activity especially during heightened REM sleep episodes. Our dreams offer "meaningful images, metaphors, and symbolism through which we may come to better understand ourselves and our relationships," writes Linda C. Senn, author of *The Many Faces of Journaling*. Dream journaling "has assisted me in working out my problems," says Toronto journaler Vanessa Rottner. Dream journals can provide a good "exercise for reflection."

—Nature Journals

Nature journals can help you learn more about the environment around you and ultimately about yourself. Because our observations on our environment reflect who and what we are, these reflections can help us discover what we value.

If you are interested in nature, such a journal can provide an excellent record of your observations and thoughts over the years and can enhance your own observational abilities, descriptive writing skills and the natural poetry of your existence. Many famous naturalists like John Muir, John James Audubon, William Healy Dall, etc. kept journals. They reflected on what they saw through writing, sketches, rubbings, poetry and inclusion of samples too! For instance, they included pressed flowers or leaves, feathers and seeds, pictures of places, etc.

For more details on how to make daily entries with examples, check Chapter 3.

—Transition Journal

In a transition journal you record the transition

you're going through, such as changing schools, moving to another street or town, job hunting or loss, starting something new. You document changing patterns in your life and what they mean to you, your reactions and how they make you feel. It is helpful to include your expectations, fears and hopes as you encounter change in your life. You might ask yourself questions like: "what do I enjoy and not enjoy?", "what do I expect for the future in what I'm doing now?", "who is most important to me now and why?"

—Grief or Trauma Journal

Grief or Trauma journals help you to express your grief, which is a very real need. As with the Transition Journal, this type of journal can help you through a difficult time or event. Keeping a grief journal can help you to heal by finding meaning in your life. If you are sincere and truthful about recording your feelings, it can help you assess your situation, find answers to confusing questions and dilemmas, understand those close to you better, and provide solace, even perspective. See Chapter 4 for more details on this kind of journal).

—Memoir or Journaling for the Next Generation

The memoir is a storyteller's journal, meant to be shared with others, whether it's your family or the world. This kind of journal is more like a summary or compendium of several journals you may have kept, themed or general, along with a relevant collection of memorabilia, scrapbook of photos, and other associated materials. Your "memoir" differs from your "memoirs", which is an autobiography of your life; a memoir focuses on just one themed segment of your life. Examples include: your changing relationship with either parent; how your trip to Australia altered your life; the influence of a teacher or mentor. A memoir is a themed accounting of part of your life; it is focused on a particular area or time that is important in your life journey. For instance, you may have kept nature journals throughout your various trips and places you lived. A memoir would collate these into a themed narrative.

Depending on who you are creating the memoir for, its form can take on a range of formats from the homespun look of a scrapbook-journal or a polished text with photos to a blog or web-based ebook. You may create and share your memoir with family and friends or publish a version for wider distribution.

2.6 Layout & Design

Lives of great men all remind us we can make our lives sublime, and, departing, leave behind us footprints in the sands of time—Henry Wadsworth Longfellow

Once you decide on the type of journal you are going to write, it makes sense to spend a little time on layout and design. A little planning and organization in the beginning can significantly influence the outcome of how your journal looks, and ultimately how it feels to you each time you open it, and whether it keeps you interested for long after you've made your entries. I still pore over my earlier journals, which I devoted some time in their design.

Things to consider in layout and design include choosing:

- the appearance & organization of your journal, which includes cover and interior

- your style and "voice" (how you narrate)

—Appearance & Organization

Things to consider in the appearance and organization of your journal include the following:

- **Cover:** you can keep it simple or personalize your paper journal cover. You may wish for a simple design if you don't want to bring undue attention to your journal. If this isn't an issue, a personalized design will make it a lot more fun and attractive, as well as easy to find.

- **Interior:** choices include color of ink used (e.g., you can vary the color according to your mood and feelings: greens and browns have an organic nature feel; blue conveys confidence and serenity; orange is fun; black and grey is elegant, lasting and wealthy looking); use of bullets and numbers for lists, alignment, use of tables and charts, inclusion of other materials and quotes.

- **Titles and subtitles:** these include how to include the date; consideration of whether to use printing vs. longhand in handwriting kinds of fonts in computer-generated narrative; using CAPs, italics or bold; using color and other ways to enhance script; inclusion of avatar or thumbnail picture, quote or other symbol with the title.

- **Margins and spaces:** this includes top, bottom and side margins as well as the spaces between paragraphs and sections. In an idea journal I kept for a medieval fantasy book I was writing, I adopted the image of an iron cross to separate thoughts in my text. The cross served as an attractive separator of two thought-streams and made the journal more attractive and interesting for later reading.

- **Use of graphics, photos and other inserted material:** this includes how and where they are placed, and whether you want to be consistent or not, use of captions, size. In one of my idea journals (for a book I was writing), I placed a thumbnail picture of the heroine on the left of each major topic heading.

—Style & "Voice"

How you write your journal will, of course, depend on your own personal "voice" but also on the type of journal and the subject matter (narrative voice). There are as many styles of narrative as there are writers. Just a few include: stream-of-conscious, random, logical, journalistic, personal letter, analytical, and fiction-style. Your writing voice is part of your writing style. "Voice" refers simply to how you write, what words you choose and how you use them. "Voice" identifies your philosophy, attitude and education to your personal feelings, prejudices and desires.

In *The Writer's Guide to Good Style* Katherine Lapworth created a voice chart to help writers figure out their voice. Her list included words like:

conservative	matter-of-fact	cheerful	humorous
quirky	serious	caring	sympathetic
trendy	funky	professional	upbeat
apologetic	unapologetic	provocative	formal
informal	friendly	reserved	edgy

—Consider Your Audience

Consider who your audience will be. You will write differently depending on whether:

- **You are writing therapeutically:** just to get something out of your head and down on paper without the wish or need to reread it (e.g., "Bugger! Bugger! Bugger! I hate that cow for stealing my idea and making it into a bestseller! I hope she gets a fatal case of writer's block and logolepsy!")

- **You are writing solely for yourself:** to read later and reflect and learn (e.g., "It's a beautiful sunny day out there but I'm in here, in a hospital room with Tom. He is lucky to be alive. Why did he ignore me and go out swimming in the rapids? Now our holiday is ruined...Why am I so angry? I should feel compassion for him, but I'm angry ...")

• **You are writing to share with others:** (e.g., "Have you ever received a gift that you didn't at first appreciate? Perhaps you didn't even realize that it was a gift. In fact you thought it was the opposite. When a volcanic dust plume from the Eyjafjallajokull Volcano disrupted air traffic all around the world on April 15th no one thought to call it a gift.")

2.7 Using Mixed Media

Painting is just another way of keeping a diary—Pablo Picasso

One of the coolest things about keeping a journal is its potential versatility. Your journal can accommodate for all kinds of expression, limited only by your imagination. You don't need to restrict your journal to writing text when you can use images, memorabilia, souvenirs, media clippings, clip art, sketches, designs and hyperlinks to video, articles and sites to express yourself.

Most cell phones have digital photo managing applications with the capacity to email or download to your computer via its own photo app, for print-out to paste into a paper journal or add to your computer or online journal.

It's wise during the planning stages of your journal, whether online or on paper, to consider the kinds of materials you might wish to include. You may need to research the needs of these supporting materials and their effect on your journal (and audience, if relevant). These might include considering things like, for example:

• memory and navigation requirements for video or photos on a blog or website

• structural requirements of nature samples in a paper journal

I discuss using mixed media in more depth in Chapter 3.

2.8 Find the Right Time and Place to Write

Look and you will find it—what is unsought will go undetected—Sophocles

Be realistic about your daily schedules, routines and inclinations and pick a time and place accordingly. Write often and try to be consistent. It's actually best to create a routine related to both time and place; the key is to be realistic about it.

■ Find a Sacred Time

Finding the time to write in your journal is critical to making entries and continuing the process. If you don't dedicate time to write you won't. Believe me, you won't. Remember what my friend Laura DeSalvo said about finding the time to write. Writing of any kind is a commitment you make to yourself. So, find a time that's right for you. If you're a morning person, don't pick the end of the day when you don't function as well to make entries. Instead, pick the early morning to write, a time before everyone else gets up and the day's distractions pile up.

It's actually best to create a routine related to time of the day (e.g., a fixed time such as every morning or right after supper) or based on some other constant in your life, say the school calendar or your daily activities. The key is to be realistic about the time(s) you've chosen. In other words, your goals should be realistic and realizable.

—Find Your Own Rhythm

There's no rule for when and how often you write in your journal. Because frequency and schedule of writing depends on the kind of journal you keep (e.g., personal diary vs. nature or trip journal) and on your own rhythms, you must decide what works best for the kind of journal you're keeping and how you operate.

With regard to the personal journal/diary, most journalists recommend that you commit to a regular writing schedule that is realistic to your overall routine and biorhythms. Some recommend you only write in the morning, after a refreshing sleep; others suggest

you write at night, at the end of the day when your memories are fresher with the day's activities. Yet others suggest you take time out during the day to jot down experiences as close to the time as they happen, then spend some time at the end of the day compiling them in your journal.

In the end, it's up to you to choose what works for you and your own rhythms. When is the best time for you to write? Once you find it, stick to that schedule.

Most recommend that you write often and try to write daily. "Don't skip writing sessions!" many also say. If you don't know what to write about just start with a rough paragraph (use the prompts provided in Chapter 3) and keep developing it.

Others suggest that you write only when something meaningful occurs in your day and don't fret if you skip days or even weeks between entries. It is less important to write daily than to write with feeling, they attest. If all you're writing is mundane happenings of no significance just to meet your daily quota, you will rob your journal of its meaning, dilute it with meaningless or boring "drivel"; you may begin to think of writing as a chore and even resent it. Because your journal is an extension of you and your feelings, it is more important to commit to honest and meaningful expression than to simply write to write. I'm inclined to agree.

If you end up skipping a day, week, or month, don't fret or feel guilty; just go ahead and create. Don't let guilt or lack of memory stop you from writing. Start from "now" and move on. I cover this topic more in Chapter 4.

■ Find a Sacred Place

Finding the perfect place(s) to write in your journal is important to creating meaningful entries. Journal writing is a reflective activity that requires the right environment for you. The best environment is a quiet one with no interruptions and where you are alone. A reflective environment will let you relax, find a connection with yourself and your feelings. You need a place where you can relax and not worry about someone barging in or other things distracting you from your thoughts. You should also feel physically comfortable and the place should meet your time requirements.

Because the suitability of a place can change with the time of day, learn the rhythms that affect the place you wish to write in. For example, the kitchen may be the center of activity during the day but an oasis of quietude during the evening. Similarly, learn what kind of environment stimulates and nurtures your writing. Does music help or do you need complete quiet? Do you respond to nature's soft breezes and sounds or do you prefer to surround yourself with the anonymous murmur of a crowded café for company?

Places that work for me include the local coffee shop, a park near my house, a library or other quiet place where I can enjoy uninterrupted anonymity. Where you write may reflect what you're writing and vice versa. To some extent, you are environment and environment is you. You might try a few places first and see what happens to the content of your entries. Entries you make while sitting under an apple tree in the breeze hearing the birds singing may differ from entries you make while sitting in your living room by the crackling fireplace with music playing or sitting at your desk in your bedroom in total silence or in a crowded café surrounded by cheerful bustle. I give more details on how to feed the muse in Chapter 4.

2.9 Networking With Your Internet Community

The information you get today is coming more and more through your friends and through your social network. It's being distributed through channels of trust and the trust isn't necessarily the BBC or The New York Times. It's people—B.J. Fogg

The Internet links you with the entire planet in ways open to and restricted only by your imagination. Blogging and participating in forums or other social networks on the Internet are two ways to interact with like-minded people of a global community. You can access social networks through any device that connects you to the Internet: your desktop or laptop computer; smart phone; tablet or notebook computer.

Social networking has freed us from the limitations of geography. It doesn't matter anymore what side of the river you live on, or what you look like. *What's important is your mind and your heart.* Social networks are an amazing way to meet and form meaningful relationships with people of similar in-terests, worldviews and minds. They provide an even playing ground for minds to interact. I know of several people who formed a relationship online through a social network and have gone on to meet in

person and become great friends. I have done it too.

Social networks allow you to keep in touch with current friends, reconnect with old ones or create new friends through similar interests or groups. Groups and forums provide easy access that helps members share. Some networks also provide good contacts for finding jobs or establishing business contacts. You can join clubs with member-ship all around the world based on a similar interest like movies, travel, music, or cycling, etc. In addition to blogs and forums, most social networking websites offer additional features that allow members to express themselves. These include the ability to design a personalized profile page complete with music, video and links. Videos can include everything from member– generated videos on hundreds of subjects to TV clips and movie trailers.

■ Popular Social Networking Sites in 2012

Some of the most popular social networking sites as of March 2012 (according to eBizMBA) include: *Facebook, Twitter, LinkedIn, MySpace, Google+, DeviantART, LiveJournal, Bebo, Friendster, Tagged,*

Pinterest, Orkut, Hi5, perfSpot, Zorbia, CafeMom, Ning, MeetUp, MyLife, MyYearBook, Netlog, Habbo, Tumblr, Yelp and *Badoo.*

▪ What's the Right Social Network For You?

With so many sites emerging on the Internet, it's a good idea to take some time to evaluate which one(s) you want to join according to your personality, interests, and goals. Six criteria developed by *TopTen Reviews* can help you evaluate a social network:

1. **Your profile:** The heart and soul of social networking sites are user's personal profiles. It's like your own Internet sanctuary, a place where you can express your thoughts and feelings, post photographs and show off your network of friends. The most popular social network websites put a strong emphasis on the user's profile, making it easy to use yet still reflect the user's personality. Look for things like profile editing, custom skins, photos, blog/journal, etc.

2. **Security:** The Internet can be a dangerous place to post personal information. All social networks should provide the ability to set profiles to private in some way. Users should also have the ability to report and block users.

3. **Networking features:** A good social network goes above and beyond just allowing users to post profiles and update pictures. Additional features should include music sections, video uploads, groups and more. Look for things like chat rooms, instant messaging, tags, bulletins, groups, forums, etc.

4. **Search:** One object of a social network is to find friends and expand relationships. Top social networking websites allow members to search for other members in a safe environment. Common search functions include search by name, city, school and email address.

5. **Help/support:** Most social network sites are self-explanatory. However, users should still be able to contact the Webmaster and/or access answers in a FAQs section.

6. **Legitimate friend focus:** The growing trend for social networks is to communicate and keep in touch with people you already know. No one wants to be inundated with unsolicited spam friend requests. The best social network sites keep profiles and search options private enough that the only people that can find you are the ones actually looking for users in their own school or neighborhood networks. Even with a completely public profile, users shouldn't be bothered with more than a couple of unsolicited comments or messages.

TopTen Reviews ranked the top ten social networking sites based on these six criteria for 2012. Sites included: *Facebook, MySpace, Bebo, Friendster, HI5,*

Orkut, Perfspot, Zorpia, Netlog, and *Habbo.*

Notably missing from this ranked list are *Google+, Pinterest, Twitter* and *LinkedIn*—all sites that have recently shown a mercurial growth in popularity and vying for a top ten position. The table below gives the pros and cons and rated verdicts for these top ten ranked social networks rated by *TopTen Reviews*:

Reviewer Rating of Top Ten Social Network Sites in 2012

	Pros	Cons	Verdict
Facebook	Users can post pictures, blogs, comments, and apps, and feel safe.	lacks interface customization options	**** reigns as the go-to site for staying in touch
MySpace	The ability to upload and share video, audio and image files as well as a blog.	Mixes personal and professional too much to work well for either.	**** lives up to its reputation with a comprehensive feature set, massive global community, and thriving music scene.
Bebo	You can personalize your profile, add apps, set privacy settings and join groups.	Navigation and friend finding on Bebo is a bit difficult.	*** a UK sensation that is gaining ground in the United States.
Friendster	You can customize your profile page with skins, photos and videos	Their FAQ section could stand to be more intuitive.	*** an excellent social networking site with lots of networking features.
Hi5	completely advertisement free.	Disappointed with their difficult search options, limited help and support section and dependency on apps.	*** has a variety of features such as chat rooms, groups and profile customization.

	Pros	Cons	Verdict
Orkut	Orkut includes a fun "ask a friend" feature that allows you to post a question and get responses from your friends.	Tthe help section is well done; however, we would have liked to see an email contact just in case.	*** your typical social networking site still in infancy
PerfSpot	PerfSpot has an eclectic collection more than 100 groups to join and free online storage for documents.	We felt that there wasn't enough attention or focus geared toward networking with people you already know.	*** offers videos, music, customizable profiles, applications, groups and you can even open your own Internet store.
Zorpia	Zorpia has an impressive music section and effective security settings to restrict access to your profile.	Unnerved by the number of unsolicited messages received from random strangers while our profile was set for public viewing.	***On the whole, Zorpia is your typical social network but boasts a large and fun international community.
Habbo	We felt completely safe using Habbo. With just a little Internet savvy young teens could have a lot of fun using this site.	Would have liked a few more customized privacy settings.	** Geared toward teens, Habbo encourages you to meet new people by mixing gaming and chat rooms using avatars.

Reference: Top Ten Reviews http://social-networking-websites-review.toptenreviews.com/

So many social networking sites and services continue to emerge on the Internet that a comprehensive listing or review of them here would be dated by the time this book was published. So, what I've done instead is talk about some of the most popular sites that also represent the kinds of social sharing/journaling sites currently on the Internet.

—Facebook

Since its launch at Harvard University in 2004,

Facebook's membership has swollen to over 900 million people, beating out *MySpace*, *LinkedIn* (a site for professionals), and *Twitter*.

I started my *Facebook* account in 2007, and confess I was initially on there daily, trying out all the applications, and I mean ALL of them, even the silly ones. I was trading messages, pokes, virtual gifts, insults , and all kinds of stuff with old and new friends. Back then, most of my existing close friends weren't on

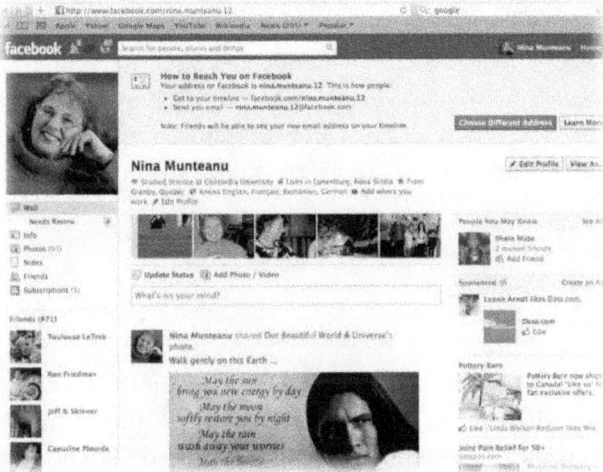

Facebook yet—they didn't even know it existed—and I networked mostly with business colleagues and blogging friends from all over the world, many who I had never met. I had also joined three blogging communities, *MyBlogLog* and *Blog Catalog* and *StumbleUpon*. All three provided me with access to other like-minded people who also authored blogs. It was, in fact, this community of bloggers who I later met again on *Facebook*, after we'd already established a good friendship through our blogs and associated networking community.

Facebook is a network that works best for people

who already know each other. I don't find it a good place to meet a stranger, because it isn't focused enough and doesn't provide adequate filters. It's like meeting someone at the local bar—without the benefit of having a drink! Now, where's the fun in that? I'd much rather meet that person face-to-face, where all my senses are able to exercise themselves. That's what I like about the blogging communities (see below): everyone there is a blogger like me and I can go to their blog to find out an awful lot about whether they're interesting and worth me sharing an online relationship with them. My son belongs to a social network devoted to skiing. Of course, it isn't just about the sport; it's a sub-culture. That social network has allowed him to find a group of cool friends who share his passion, and speak the same language.

—Google+

Google+ aims to make sharing on the web more like sharing in real life. It features the "Stream", "Circles", "Messenger", "Hangouts", and "Sparks" and "Games" (among other apps). Said to be rivaling *Facebook*, this social network has become very popular lately. Mark Sullivan of PC World says that the main reason why *Google+* is gaining a lot of ground as a social network site is its integration. Google is building social networking features and tools into almost all of its existing online services from Search to Documents to Video (*YouTube*).

"*Google+* is already integrated into the navigation bar at the top right of almost all Google products; this lets you monitor all *Google+* events (updates, messages, etc.) as well as share content with friends without ever leaving the Google service you happen to be using. Millions and millions of people use Google's free services (Gmail, Docs, Search, etc.), and with *Google+* bound so tightly to them it may start to seem silly to jump out to some other site (*Facebook*) to do your social networking."

Here's what one user shared: "Google offers everything I need and most things I want out of communicating with people over the net. I am totally over *FB* (and *Skype* for that matter) and will be looking to jump head-on into the world of Google. With Google I have email, chat, video/voice calls, social networking, document suite, search, photos and videos and more...why bother with multiple apps, services and websites for these things?"

—LinkedIn

LinkedIn was launched in 2003 as a business social network, It's used by most members to professionally network and socialize via "connections". It features a number of apps and where you can post your resume and other information about your business. If you're looking for a job, this is a great community of professionals to network, socialize and get work. I landed a great writing coach contract recently through an online group forum there.

■ Micro-Blogging

—Twitter

Twitter describes itself as a micro-blog and social networking service. It lets users send and read text-based posts up to 140 characters, known as "tweets". Launched in 2006, the service rapidly gained worldwide popularity, with over 300 million users as of 2011, generating over 300 million tweets and handling over 1.6 billion search queries a day. Since its launch, *Twitter* has become one of the top sites visited on the Internet and considered the top SMS (short message system) of the Internet. *Twitter* recently gained importance, along with *Facebook* and *YouTube*, in helping to organize and publicize international social protest movements like *Arab Spring* and *Occupy Wall Street* in 2010 and 2011.

—Tumblr

Tumblr is a free microblog hosting platform and social networking website that offers professional and customizable templates, "bookmarklets", photos, videos and mobile apps. You can post multimedia and other content to a short-form blog, named a "tumblelog", creating a rich and unique profile that fully expresses your individuality. You can share with the public or make your blog private. Much of the website's features are accessed from the "dashboard" interface, where the option to post content and posts of followed blogs appear.

—Pinterest

Pinterest is a visual bookmarking site launched in 2010. It describes itself as an online pinboard to organize and share things you love. It recently emerged as one of the top websites in the Social Networking & Forums category. There's something for everyone, although the site is dominated by images featuring home décor, crafts, fashion, and food. Over half of the visitors are women and 60% percent between the ages of 25 and 44. One blogger describes why he thinks *Pinterest* has become so popular: "*Pinterest* is...moving mechanisms for content sharing beyond connections (friends) and towards relevance, effectively broadening the social horizon for us content addicts."

■ Blogging

Blogs—short for weblogs—have been on the Internet since the 1990s. Blogs are basically discussion or information sites published on the World Wide Web that consist of discrete entries (called posts), typically displayed in reverse chronological order so the most recent post appears first. Until 2009, blogs were usually the work of one person or small group, and were often themed on a single subject. More recently "multi-author blogs" (MABs) have developed, with posts written by large numbers of authors and professionally edited. Blog traffic from MABs includes newspapers, media outlets, universities, interest groups and various large

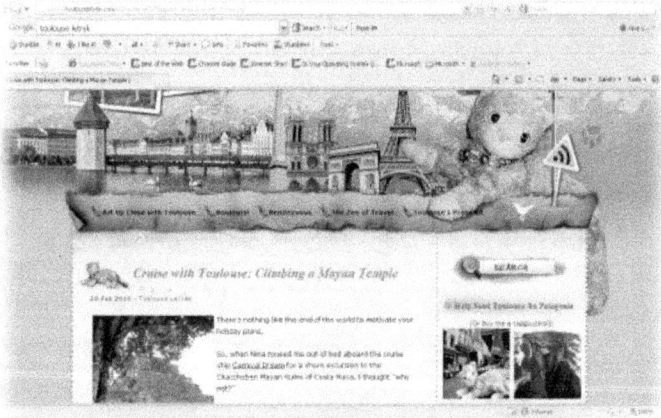

organizations wanting to share, advertise and sell something. Many are associated with a large corporation and often reflect corporate propaganda.

The individual and personal blog remains one of the most versatile and satisfying methods of self-expression and interaction on the Internet.

In 2007 I started my blog *The Alien Next Door* as my ongoing musings in the fields of writing, the environment and pop culture. It has steadily risen in popularity from its humble origins and now attracts over four hundred viewers daily from over two hundred countries with as many as two hundred comments per post. The key to blogs is dialogue.

If sharing and discussing your views, philosophies, interests and theories is important to you, blogs can provide you with an international platform that sweeps across cultural and geographical barriers. With a blog, the world is truly your oyster.

Some of the most popular blog platforms include: *Wordpress; Blogger; Blog.com; TypePad Micro; Jux; Tumblr; Blogetery; Posterous Spaces; LiveJournal;* and *Weebly.*

I talk more about this form of online sharing in Chapter 3.

—Discovery Engines & Info-Sharing Sites

StumbleUpon, Delicious, Digg, Readit, are just a few of the many collaborative tagging sites that house communities of users who rank and share sites or items they like. They form communities in which people share what they like and why. They are basically clubs and there is one for just about any interest out there from travel (*Trip Advisor*) to books (e.g., *Goodreads* and *LibraryThing*).

—Other Social Media-Sharing Sites

Other social media sharing and archiving sites include mixed media images and video. Some of the most popular platforms include *YouTube, Vimeo, Metacaf, BlipTV,* free sites for video and *Flickr, Smugmug, Picassa, Phanfare, Zenfolio, Photobucket, Divvyshot,* and *DeviantART* for still images.

Sites like *Tumblr* and *Pinterest* integrate visual bookmarking of images with text, links, video and anything else that permits self-expression of "identity". The popularity of these multi-media social sharing sites reflects our need to connect. It is a new form of creativity and should be considered a bona fide art form.

—You're Less Likely to Get Sick If You Actively Socialize

Isn't that an oxymoron? More sociable people are more exposed to germs, after all. Yet a study by

Sheldon Cohen and his colleagues pub-lished in *Psych-ological Science* (2003) showed that less sociable people caught colds more often than those who socialized. While that doesn't follow the straight logic of exposure, it sheds light on the concept of mind-body dualism and the link between physical and mental health. People who socialize have a social identity, possibly multiple social identities, which seems to make them more resilient.

"Belonging to social groups and networks

appears to be an important predictor of health—just as important as diet and exercise," says a September/October 2009 article in *Scientific American Mind* by Jetten et.al. Socializing makes us healthier and more resilient. A 2005 study by Bernadette Boden-Albala at Columbia University found that socially isolated patients were twice as likely to have another stroke within five years as were those with meaningful social relationships. In fact, being cut off from others put people at far greater risk of another stroke than traditional factors like having coronary artery disease or being physically inactive, said the report.

Karen Ertel and colleagues at the Harvard School of Public Health, who tracked a large group of elderly Americans over sixty years, found "significantly less memory loss in those who were more socially integrated and active." (*American Journal of Public Health*).

Does virtual socializing (e.g., social networking through *Facebook*, *MySpace*, blogging and chat-lines) contribute to better health like the examples above? That's what researchers are still asking and some speculate that social networking provides a good socializing venue, particularly for those of us who are less mobile or otherwise more isolated from loved ones and close friends (through travel, for instance). But, researchers also suggest that this venue does not provide a totally satisfying substitute for face-to-face real-world engagement. It comes down to a healthy balance based on circumstance. Now more than ever, we have options for meeting new people, joining groups of like-minds (whether virtual or real) where we can safely be challenged and excited by life, associations

that provide us with fulfilling activities and good mental health. I am an active blogger and online communicator (I travel a lot and find online chatting a wonderful way to keep in touch with family, friends and colleagues). I have also formed many associations through this venue, several of whom I have since met face-to-face and forged close friendships with.

That is, in the final analysis, the point: good mental health. You create your reality. Now, go socialize!

2.10 References

Algren, Nelson. 1958-1988. In: Plimpton, George (ed.): "Writers at Work". (8 vols). Secker & Warburg. London, UK.

Berry, Wendell. 1990. "What are People For?" North Point Press. San Francisco, CA.

Byrne, Rhonda. 2012. "The Magic". Atria Books. New York, NY.

Chandler, Daniel. 1987. Are We Ready for Word-Processors? *English in Australia* 79: 11-17.

Chandler, Daniel. 1992. "The Phenomenology of Writing by Hand". *Intelligent Tutoring Media* 3(2/3): 65-74.

Jetten, J. et al. 2009. "The Social Cure?". *Scientific American Mind*. September/October Issue, 2009.

Lapworth, Katherine. 2011. "The Writer's Guide to Good Style. A Teach Yourself Book". Hodder Education. London, UK.

Munteanu, Nina. 2009. "You're Less Likely to Get Sick if You Actively Socialize". *The Alien Next Door*: http://sfgirl-thealiennextdoor.blogspot.ca/2009/11/youre-less-likely-to-get-sick-if-you.html

Munteanu, Nina. 2010. "To Facebook or Not to Facebook: What's the Right Social Network For You?" *The Alien Next Door*. http://sfgirl-thealiennextdoor.blogspot.ca/2010/02/to-facebook-or-not-to-facebook-whats.html

Ross, Margaret. 2012. Registered Clinical Counsellor with Calm Waters Counseling, New Westminster, B.C.

Personal communication.

Selfe, Cynthia. 1985. "The Electronic Pen: Computers and the Composing Process". In: Collins, James & Elizabeth A. Sommers (eds), "Writing On-line: Using Computers in the Teaching of Writing". Upper Montclair, NJ. Boynton/Cook.

Senn, Linda C. 2001. "The Many Faces of Journaling: Topics & Techniques for Personal Journal Writing".

Chapter 3: GETTING STARTED

The beginning is the most important part of the work—
Plato

3.1 What's Inside an Entry?

What lies behind us and what lies before us are tiny matters, compared to what lies within us— Ralph Waldo Emerson

Every entry you make should start with the date and time. This becomes important when you return to a particular entry and wish to know when you wrote it in context with your greater journey.

Each entry should record thoughts and associated feelings of the day (these two should accompany each other; they are a pair—one without the other has little meaning to you when you revisit the entry). Include events that affected you in some way and discuss why. Include both the joys and the heartaches.

It is very important that you be honest when writing your journal entry. "Write how you *really* feel and not how you think you *should* feel," says Klug (2002). "Record what you *really* think, not what you believe you *ought* to think."

There are advantages to making your entry as

close to the time of the experience as possible (Holly, 1989). You can jot down things as you encounter them with a mobile digital device or a small mobile notebook. Then at the end of the day you can download or transpose your notes and fill in the details in your computer journal or notebook journal. This gives you the advantage of recording your immediate experience and reaction as well as your reflections later on (which may be more objective and analytical) as you transpose.

3.2 "Anatomy" of an Entry

It is in the knowledge of the genuine conditions of our lives that we must draw our strength to live and our reasons for living—Simone de Beauvoir

Think of including these four basic elements when making an entry:

1. **Description/observation:** after adding the date and time, you describe the situation, encounter, experience and your feelings associated with them.

2. **Additional material/research:** any information that comes to you after the event.

3. **Reflection:** going back to the experiences, analyzing your feelings and evaluating them to learn and act. This may occur when you transpose an entry made in the field or on your mobile device into your permanent journal at home, or

4.   **Things to do:** the process of reflection may lead to several conclusions for taking action.

3.3 Structure & Organization of Entries in Your Journal

Imagination is the true magic carpet—Norman Vincent Peale

There is no rule on entry structure or organization. This is because how you organize your journal depends on how you want to use it.

For instance, you can organize your journal by 1) chronology (by date and time, as you make your entry. Entries would follow a linear timeline regardless of what subjects you are writing about) or 2) by subject (with initial entry opening the subject and subsequent entries associated with that subject nested within it— like a thread in a forum on the Internet).

Journals organized chronologically have a simple layout, based simply on your entries as you make them. The significant aspect is the date and time. In such a journal, it is easy to assess what you were doing and how you were feeling during any particular time period. Because this kind of journal is structured as the entries are made, any kind of journal works— including bound notebooks, which are not easily reorganized.

Because subject-based organization is independent of time (and therefore when entries are made), this is easier to do in a computer journal, where reorganizing and time-independent entry is easy. You can also do this fairly easily with loose-leaf pages in a binder. Notebooks don't lend themselves to time-independent entry because their pages are bound. The only way to do this is to index your chronological entries. For instance, say you opened with an entry about starting a new job. You could tag that entry with

a green tab and any subsequent entries to do with the new job could be similarly tagged. Then, say your next entry was about how you met an interesting person in the café and you tagged it orange. Any entries related to that person and your developing friendship would be tagged orange.

3.4 "Once Upon a Time..." How to Start

I myself do nothing. The Holy Spirit accomplishes all through me—William Blake

OK, so now you know what's typically inside

an entry and have some ideas on how to organize them in your journal. You've defined a sacred time and place to write and you've decided on the kind of journal you're going to write. You have your tools in front of you and you're ready to begin. You've opened to the first page in your journal or have the computer screen ready in front of you.

Start writing.

For most of us starting anything new can be the hardest part. That's why I gave you the previous chapter on what to do before you get started. Being prepared always helps.

Still need some help getting started? Here are some suggestions...

■ Use Lead-in Sentences

In his book *The Tao of Writing* Ralph L. Wahlstrom suggests that if you have problems getting started—particularly in a personal daily journal—one way is to focus on a question or lead-in sentence appropriate to your day. Here are some general lead-in sentences that can work for you in a number of circumstances about values, dreams and aspirations:

- Happiness is...
- The best things about me (or someone else) are...
- What's bothering me is...
- What puzzled me today was...
- School (or my job) isn't very satisfying lately...
- The things I value the most are...
- So-and-so really upset me...
- Today was beautiful because...

A clear and relevant lead-in sentence can inspire you to continue into areas you would never have imagined.

—State of Mind

Here are a few examples of prompts for your state of mind:

- I am happy because...
- I am bored because
- I am tired because...
- I am angry because...
- I am pleased with myself because...
- I fee gratitude for...

—Memories

Here are a few examples of prompts for memories:

- A house you once lived in
- My first sight of the ocean
- The first smell I can remember
- My favorite teacher
- My most embarrassing moment
- A cherished relative (grandmother, uncle, nephew, etc.)
- An inspiring mentor
- A keystone event or accomplishment
- An event surrounding a favorite pet

■ Ask Questions

Ron Klug (2002) provides a series of starter questions to help prompt your end-of-the-day journal entry. I've taken them and added some of my own here:

- As I look back on the day, what were the most significant events (and why)?
- In what ways was this day unique, different from other days?
- Did I have any particular meaningful conversations?
- How did I feel during the day? What were the emotional highs and lows?
- Did I find myself worrying about anything?
- Why have I felt so sad these last few days?...
- Why was so-so mean to me today?...
- What were the chief joys of the day? What did I accomplish?
- Did I fail at anything? What can I learn from this?
- What did I learn today?
- When did I feel most alive?

Try to work through the questions. Don't worry about being off-the-wall or wrong, says Wahlstrom. "The most outrageous answers to the silliest questions can offer insight."

—What If...

Exploring fantasy scenarios can be fun. One day my son shared with me that as he and his friends walked to school together he would ask them a "what if" question, which prompted quality discussion all the way to the school and helped them to get to know each other and themselves better. "What if you won a million dollars?...What would you do?" "What if you were an animal? Which one would you be?" "What if you could choose to go back in history? Where would you go and why?"

Here are some example "What if" prompts:

- What if I decided to be a cartoonist and write graphic novels...?
- What if I time traveled to the future...?
- What if I found an old watch on the ground that told the time in the future...?
- What if the world was going to end and I had an ark...?
- What if I lived in Paris...?
- What if I was an eagle or a superhero...?

You can be as outlandish and fantastical as you want. The idea is to spark the muse to write. Pick something fun and relevant.

■ Make a List

Making and keeping lists can be very satisfying. Lists help us organize our minds and help us see our progress in a day. Lists like checklists for a daily, weekly or other type of activity can be not only fulfilling in that they show our progress in our activities and tasks, but they serve as a record we can later look back on. Here are some examples of kinds of lists you can start:

- Assets and liabilities (your own and others)
- Priority to do lists with comments

- Life lists (list the events of your life to do with a specific theme like marriages, children, relationships, education, friends & enemies, etc.)
- Book list (books you want to read, you have read want to reread and why)
- Sites, sounds and smells
- List of heroes in your life (real and literary)
- List of what you've accomplished and want to
- "Bucket List"
- Places you want to travel to or live and why
- Fantasy List (what you would do if you won a million dollars)

■ Write a "Letter" or Have a Dialogue

Start with a list of people who have been important to you (they could even be a fictional character or no longer living, or your unborn child). Choose one and write them a letter. This helps you focus your thoughts. I remember writing a letter to my pet cat shortly after he died. It was a sweet, moving and very satisfying.

You could also have a two-sided conversation between yourself and a chosen person (real or unreal). The person could be someone you admire or someone you are having difficulties with. You can have a dialogue with a part of your body, with an animal or plant or anything you choose to animate with interactive abilities. Use your imagination and have fun.

▪ Write About Nothing in Particular

Wahlstrom tells us that "some of our greatest insights come to us in unguarded moments, when we have no topic, no agenda. In the spirit of *Wu Wei*, we often accomplish the most when we do the least." Remember not to worry about grammar or sentence structure. Let your thoughts flow, unencumbered by the structures you have learned in school.

▪ Don't Let Fear Stop You Before You Even Begin

"Many of us are afraid to write about what we really feel or believe," says Wahlstrom. This is because we fear that we will offend someone or show our weaknesses to them, even to ourselves. "As we write for self-discovery," Wahlstrom adds, "we may discover (or uncover) bits of ourselves that we'd rather leave buried." He counsels us to remember two things:

1.   Only by bringing these hidden artifacts into full sunlight will you see them clearly enough to deal with them; and,

2.   Rarely are our deepest secrets and desires unusual, deviant or extraordinary. They are ultimately what make us human.

It is those very hidden aspects that, through scrutiny, can provide us with the opportunities to triumph and prevail. You cannot prevail without first revealing.

■ First Thoughts...

In her book *Writing Down the Bones* Natalie Goldberg (2005) offers a sound formula on not only getting your first thoughts down but on digging into the good stuff without distraction. Her suggestions pertain equally to an entry written by hand or typed on the computer. Here's her 6-step formula:

1. **Keep your hand moving**—don't pause to reread the line you have just written. That's stalling and trying to get control of what you're saying.

2. **Don't cross out**—that is editing as you write. Even if you write something you didn't mean to write, leave it.

3. **Don't worry about spelling, punctuation, grammar**—don't even care about staying within the margins and lines on the page.

4. **Lose control.**

5. **Don't think. Don't get logical.**

6. **Go for the jugular**—if something comes up in your writing that is scary or naked, dive right into it. It probably has lots of energy.

The idea behind this formula is "to burn through to first thoughts, to the place where energy is unobstructed by social politeness or the internal censor, the place where you are writing what your mind actually sees and feels, not what it thinks it should see or feel," says Goldberg.

■ "Morning Pages"

In describing her "morning pages" Julia Cameron, author of *The Artist's Way*, provides another prompt-method that relies also on stream-of-conscious writing. She describes them as "three pages of longhand writing, strictly stream-of-consciousness: *oh, God, another morning. I have NOTHING to say. I need to wash the curtains. Did I get my laundry yesterday? Blah, blah, blah....*They might also, more ingloriously be called brain drain, since that is one of their main functions." The key is to start. The rest takes care of itself. And, sometimes, that's when magic happens....

For instance, Cameron describes how on one occasion her morning pages that had started as a pastime about staring at the mountain out of her bedroom window...*a humpbacked marvel different in every weather...wrapped in clouds one day, dark and wet the next...*found a character named Johnny strolling into her pages. Without planning to, she was writing a novel!

3.5 How to Make an Entry

People who wait for a magic wand will fail to see that they ARE the magic wand— Thomas Leonard

■ How to Start on Paper

Assemble all your materials and get settled in a place with good energy. You've applied the things you read about in Chapter 2 and reviewed some of the beginning tools here in the above sections. Now it's just a question of writing. Let the flow of the pen guide you.

—Paper Journal Writing Tips

Here are some tips on how to start…and keep going:

- Relax and write what you feel; don't forget to have fun with it
- Start with something interesting (use a prompt like I give above)
- Don't take yourself too seriously
- Remember that you can make mistakes
- Take your time
- It's ok to make a mess

■ How to Start on Your Computer

Starting your journal on your computer is much like starting one on paper. The only difference is that you are typing on a screen versus writing on lined or blank paper. The beginning part is still the same. You are faced with a blank screen. Use the same prompts you would for paper.

You have more options on your computer with its connections to the Internet. Just as you would use a book of quotes to help give you prompts, you can access various sources on the Internet to find inspirational quotes, links or even reminders. Remember to bookmark your favorite sites that you will wish to use again for inspiration.

■ How to Start Online

Writing online is like being on the radio. You know you're broadcasting to "the world"; but it doesn't feel like it, because no one is tangibly visible. You sit alone in the sound booth and talk to...well yourself (and your millions of listeners by default). That is both the empowering and scary aspect of radio: it provides a feeling of intimacy (and privacy, even) even though you are exposing yourself to potential millions. The Internet has a way of doing that. We share on Facebook or blog about a personal event and, because we are alone when we write, a part of us feels like we still are alone even though once we've pushed the send or "print" button we've just posted to a bazillion people.

The oxymoron of communicating on the Internet—whether it's a blog, or a social network—is that it feels intimate while being public. This is both scary and wonderful. Exposure always is.

—Lose Your Fear but Keep Your Senses

Writing online is potentially all-powerful and humbling. You are potentially sharing with the entire world. It's thrilling. It's also scary.

There's a poignant scene near the end of the 2005 movie "Coach Carter" where a student finally responds to Carter's insistent question of "what is your deepest fear?". It is a quote often mistakenly attributed to Nelson Mandela but originally written by Marianne Williamson ("A Return to Love: Reflections on the Principles of A Course in Miracles"). And it speaks to the artist in all of us:

"Our deepest fear is not that we are inadequate. Our deepest fear is that we are powerful beyond measure. It is our light, not our darkness that most frightens us. We ask ourselves, Who am I to be brilliant, gorgeous, talented, fabulous? Actually, who are you *not* to be? You are a child of God. Your playing small does not serve the world. There is nothing enlightened about shrinking so that other people won't feel insecure around you. We are all meant to shine, as children do. We were born to make manifest the glory of God that is within us. It's not just in some of us; it's in everyone. And as we let our own light shine, we unconsciously give other people permission to do the same. As we are liberated from our own fear, our presence automatically liberates others."

Let me tell you a story...I've been writing stories since I was ten years old. I used to stay up until late at night telling stories with my sister, when our parents were snoring in bed: fantastical stories with a cast of thousands and spanning the entire universe. When I was in my teens, I began to write a book, inspired by several dystopian movies and my own passion for saving the planet. It was called "Caged in World". By the time I was married and had my son, I had written three entire books, none of which I'd published. I had by then sold several short stories and essays and articles to mainstream, travel and science fiction magazines. I started to become known as a reviewer and critic of movies and books. And my short stories were gaining good reputation with stellar reviews and invitations to appear in anthologies.

I began to market my first book—a medical ecological thriller—to agents and publishers. Although I got many bites for partials and even full manuscripts, none came to fruition.

Then something strange happened.

Driven by something inside me, I wrote over the space of a few months a book entitled "Collision with Paradise" based on some research I'd done on Atlantis, the bible and the Great Flood. The book was important to me on a number of fronts: in its ecological message of cooperation and its exploration of new paradigms of existence. I wrote it fast and well and it hardly needed editing. Without thinking and without hesitation, I submitted it for publication. As quickly as I'd written it, I had an offer from a publisher. My first published book!

My first reaction was elation. My second reaction was: *What have I done?* I was proud of my book and its story, but it also contained erotica. My first thought was: how are my family and friends going to react? What about my parents? OMG! Fear, not of failure but of success came crashing down on me and I felt so exposed. If I could have retracted it, I might have. Thankfully, I didn't. While some friends and family did in fact shake their heads and look askance at my work (and labeled it variously), the book was very well received by critics and readers alike. It was, in fact, a hit. Faced with success, I bowed to its consequences and embraced what it brought: the good, the bad and the ugly. I was, in fact, relieved. I have many times since contemplated my actions in submitting this subversive novel that exposed me incredibly. Was it brave intuition or bold recklessness that propelled me? The point is, I'd stepped out into the light and crossed the line into another paradigm. There was no way back into the shadows. And that's good.

Just remember that when you write online, it's out there for the world to see. You can't retract it. No turning back. No taking back. I have these simple words of advice: write from the heart and be impeccable. Be that which you admire.

—Online Writing Tips

Here are some tips for writing online:

• Write your first draft and polish it on your computer or mobile device in Word or similar text file. Once you are happy with it, then transfer it to your online platform (e.g., blog, website, social network, forum, etc.). This lets you revise not only your writing but your thoughts before sharing them with the world. It also gives you the chance to polish your language and show you at your best; there is nothing like language riddled with grammatical mistakes and typos to put someone off and not take your content seriously.

• Choose your online venues carefully and share your materials in appropriate venues. For instance, you wouldn't want to share thoughts on saving the environment on a right-wing site that promotes industry at the expense of environment. Well, unless you really wanted to, that is (subversive grin).

• Review your reasons for sharing your material with the public. Some things are not meant to be shared with more than your intimate friends or family. Keep them that way by keeping them off the Internet. Be judicious about *what you share* by choosing *where you share*.

• Be mindful of how your sharing will affect close friends and family. How does it reflect you in your work, school, community, etc.? What is your public *persona*?

- Envision what someone—including you— would think of what you wrote 5 years from now or 10 years from now. Because, that's the good, bad and ugly of the Internet—things stay there...well...forever...

- Always remember that you are writing for a larger audience than you might think. Invariably, that is what happens.

- Be careful. Be impeccable. Be respectful. By showing care, respect and integrity you invite it back.

3.6 Example Steps for a Nature Journal
Forget not that the earth delights to feel your bare feet and the winds long to play with your hair—Kahlil Gibran

Here are the steps for keeping a nature journal:

1. **Decide on the kind of nature journal you want to make**: your decision should take into account whether you wish to include samples, pictures or only text. If you're using a notebook

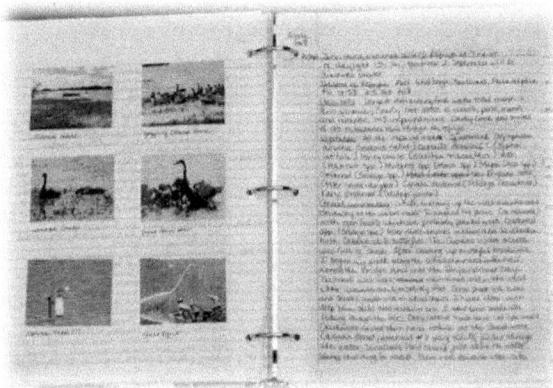

(not a computer) size is important. Keep it large enough to include what you need but small enough to be portable. You may wish to create a journal only for a specific place, topic, issue or trip (e.g., the river behind your place; local birds; recycling in your community; your trip to Tanzania or the local zoo). There are different kinds of journal styles for different uses. For instance, *Grinnell* journals are field journals used by scientists and phenology journals are specific to making field observations. If you are really serious about journaling in nature—rain or shine—you can get one with waterproof paper, like *Rite in the Rain*, or *DeckExpert. Butler Survey Supplies* also makes waterproof loose leaf paper.

2.   **Make or buy a suitable journal**: most nature journals are compiled from notebooks or notepads of plain white paper. You can get some that have one side lined for writing and the opposite side unlined for drawing, sketches and pasting in pictures or samples. Make sure your journal is sturdy and protected against the elements. Some covers are waterproof. Otherwise, it might be a good idea to carry a plastic bag with you.

3.   **Get the other equipment you need**: if you plan to make sketches or paint with watercolor or collect specimens, ensure that you have the equipment: pencils, pencil crayons, paint kit, adhesive tape, camera, other collection material. A backpack would be useful to put your journal and materials into.

4.   **Dedicate time and place to journaling**: nature journals, like most themed journals, do not need to be kept daily or on a routine. Journal entries will depend on the specific topic or area you have chosen to follow. Keep your journal handy to your journal topic. You may wish to keep it and associated materials in a dedicated backpack, handy to grab when you go on your outings. If you keep lists of things to bring on various trips or outings, include the journal.

5.   **Observe the world around you**: nature journaling relies mostly on observing and reflecting. Cultivate your observational skills by learning to quiet your mind from distractions and focusing on the subject matter. Sketching and taking pictures can help provide the focus you need as well as giving you something to put into your journal. Slow down. Stop and watch and listen. Get close. Don't be afraid to crouch and move in close. The wonders of nature are often right in front of your nose, just waiting for a new way to be seen.

6.   **Write on location**: your nature journal will be most valuable if you use it in the field to record what you see as you see it. If you rely on your memory to write in your journal later, it will be less accurate (though it might be more poetic). You are more likely to make an entry if you bring your journal with you; if you leave your journal at home and wait until later, you may not get to it and the magic of the moment may be lost. Once you get home and revisit your entry, you can confirm and elaborate on your observations in the field.

7.   **Begin each entry with location, date, time**: "where" and "when" are important pieces of information to include in any journal entry. They are particularly important in a nature journal. Time and place relate to important natural cycles like season and diurnal cycle. If your nature journal is more scientific, you may wish to include other important descriptors like weather, temperature, wind, precipitation, etc.

You may wish to leave the odd page blank as space to paste in additional information from later research related to your entry.

8. **Record observations in several ways:** regardless of whether you consider yourself a good artist or not, sketches and drawings can provide a wealth of information (that you may not have thought to add in your writing) and add an element of interest to a journal entry. Pictures are a great tool for adding accurate details to an observation. Don't be afraid to get close. All too often we take a picture, thinking the camera sees what we see (and interpret) and when we look at the photo the object of your attention is too far away or surrounded by so much "noise" it's hard to distinguish.

9. **Learn more about what you saw:** it's a good idea to confirm and elaborate your observations with research. When you go to the library or read online about what you saw, you will likely generate even more interest. This is where sketches or images or samples come in handy, particularly if you want to identify something you've seen.

10. **Revisit your past entries**: you may wish to consult a previous entry to compare with something you've just observed or use it in an experiment you're conducting. Either way, reading your nature journal can be a great learning experience and a lot of fun.

The American Museum of Natural History describes a field journal as being unique to the journalist. "There is no one way to keep a field journal," they say. "Some scientists will sketch simple pencil drawings, and others will paint colorful, detailed images. You can use whatever tools work best for you. Try working with pens, pencils or watercolors to capture an image, whether it is a view of the Moon, the veins of a leaf, or the legs of a beetle." You can record your observations with charts, list and labels, sketches, samples and photos. You can also write long, detailed descriptions.

Some questions they come up with to help prompt you include:

- "What do I see?" Some things to include are: size, shape and color, what it is doing, how it relates to other things, why it is so interesting to you.

- "Do I see anything that surprises me?"

- "How have I traveled to this spot?" This is good information for possible later visits, especially if you wish to do a series of related observations.

- "What tools do I have?" This is good to remember for later visits and to assess the appropriateness of the observation. In most scientific observations, the methods and techniques used are critical to the validity of the observation.

- "Who is with me on this expedition?" Researchers always include who was there. This helps for later consultation.

- "What time of day is it?" In the natural sciences time of day is critical because so much in nature is diurnal (e.g., responds and changes as the day changes)

While recently browsing on the Internet, I ran across a very attractive yet simple nature blog. What made Judy Butler's "Naturalist Journal: Down the Nature Trail" so appealing was her mixed use of regular text augmented with scanned handwritten pages containing color-pencil drawings and flower pressings. This charming "homespun" expression resembled a real three-dimensional journal.

3.7 Using Art, Photos and Other Media

I found I could say things with color and shapes that I couldn't say any other way – things I had no words for—
Georgia O'Keeffe

You can express yourself in art through free-form, doodling, cartooning, logos, collage, sketches, coloring, paintings, photographs and mixed media. For instance, you can create a mixed-media scrapbook-style journal with mementos, souvenirs, samples, magazine and newspaper clippings, etc. On a computer-based journal you can add links to web pages and music, images and videos. You can create slideshows, movies or other multi-media presentations.

Art also includes poetry, prose, puzzles, riddles, quotes and other forms of narrative. Using a favorite quote you ran across or found, is a good way to start an entry, particularly if you haven't anything particular to write about. Quotes can be very in-

99

spirational. For more discussion on inspirational prompts see Chapter 4.

When you include works of art in your journal or keep a journal entirely of art, you are expressing yourself metaphorically. Metaphor is an indirect language of comparison and deep truth.

■ Letting Your Art Speak To You

Whether you're working with a core theme or moving along with the questions of your everyday life journey, it is good to be mindful of the elements of design in your art: the lines, shapes and colors in your interaction with the world. These are the tools in the language of art. The art you do—whether it's taking pictures or collecting them, sketching or collecting art, composing or collecting music—can tell you a lot about how you feel and think at that moment. They can also help you discover things and work through the problems, solve issues and take action. They are the deepest reflection of you.

Marianne Hieb (2005) tells us that the principals of design include balance, movement, rhythm, contrast, emphasis, pattern and unity. Like the fabric of a fine tapestry, these principles hold aspects of creativity together and define works of art. "They are also present in your life," says Hieb, "which is the greatest work of art."

Balance: you find balance when you first walk, in riding a bike, skating and skiing. In art, balance refers to the distribution of visual weights. It is the visual equilibrium of the elements that comprise the entire image. Symmetrical balance is achieved when elements or sections of equal quality mirror each other. An example of asymmetrical balance with unequal elements would be a painting where one small intense color can balance a grouping of less intense and larger things. This provides excellent metaphor in journal representations and life-journeys. Think of the balances between irregular and simple shapes, intense and subdued colors. Think color, shape, size, texture, value when creating balance or showing the opposite. Balance can indicate movement and can also radiate out from a single point of focus.

Movement: A balance of movement and stillness exists in all works of art, in dance, in music, in painting, sculpture and literature, says Hieb. "Shapes and colors move the eye most easily through the work. Lines provide visual passage or linkage. Your eyes follow the edges of darkness or edges of light. Visual movement leads your seeing through the work, to a point of focus." Horizontal, vertical and diagonal are the three main types of visual movement. Horizontal movement usually conveys a calm or restful sense. If you use vertical movement, you may be expressing a feeling of firmness or stability or even growing. Diagonal movement often reflects action and swiftness.

Rhythm: Rhythm is the repetition of visual movement of color, shapes, lines, values, forms, spaces and textures. Movement and rhythm work together, says Hieb. Rhythms are present in all natural things and can be regular, irregular, staccato and progressive. Rhythm has the power of uniting and energizing images and themes, through implied connection and relationship.

Contrast: contrast is delivered through color, texture, and shape. Contrast creates visual excitement, drama. Says Hieb, "at the place of darkest dark, the light in contrast is the most noticeable...[in] the places of greatest contrast...grace is waiting there for you." Contrast can exist in many forms: smooth vs. rough; light vs. dark; dry vs. wet; playful vs. dour; anger vs. forgiveness—just to name a few. Contrast is drama. It is a place of potential conflict, tension, and great enlightenment.

Emphasis: Emphasis creates focus. You can emphasize color, shapes, direction or other art elements to achieve dominance, says Hieb. Given that each of these elements is significance with the psyche, what elements you chose to emphasize in your drawing or selection of art can give you additional insight to what was important to you or affecting you at the time. For instance, colors can reflect mood: red emphasizes and reflects passion or danger; green reflects nature and healing; orange is fun and warm; blue is cool and calming, etc. Shapes can be very symbolic. Researchers have shown that angular shapes are less apt to elevate feelings of comfort and well being then circular shapes, which engender feelings of safety, unity and harmony. Squares can reflect conformity and equality; triangles can suggest self-discovery and revelation; spirals can express creativity, and so on.

102

Pattern: A pattern is basically a recognizable series of elements. For instance, you experience patterns of activities and behavior. Patterns are the planned or random repetitions that occur in nature and in your life. They increase visual excitement. Patterns that occur in nature exhibit unique and exquisite beauty. Pattern—in shape, color, texture—can relate to one's history, personal experiences, and choices. They can similarly reveal our reactions, reflections and feelings.

Unity: the use of a dominant color scheme or overall surface treatment creates a strong sense of unity. Unity provides the cohesive quality that makes an artwork feel complete and finished, says Hieb. "A subjective sense of oneness is the felt experience of the principle of unity," she adds. Unity is achieved through the harmonious integration of the previous elements I named. What unity looks like will be unique to each individual and to their stage in their life journey. What does unity look like to you?

I paint not by sight but by faith. Faith gives you sight—
Amos Ferguson

3.8 References

Butler, Judith. 2009. "Naturalist Journal: Down the Nature Trail".
http://downthenaturetrail.blogspot.com/2009/08/tennessee-journal-page-elizabethton-and.html

Cameron, Julia. 1992. "The Artist's Way". Penguin Putnam Inc., New York, NY. 222pp.

Goldberg, Natalie. 2005. "Writing Down the Bones: Freeing the Writer Within". Shambhala Publications. Boston, MS. 171pp.

Hieb, Marianne. 2005. "Inner Journeying Through Art-Journaling." Jessica Kingsley Publishers, London. 176pp.

Holly, Mary Louise. 1989. "Writing to Grow. Keeping a personal-professional journal." Heinemann. Portsmouth, New Hampshire.

Klug, Ron. 2002. "How to Keep a Spiritual Journal. A guide to journal keeping for inner growth and personal discovery". Kogan Page. London.

Wahlstrom, Ralph L. 2006. "The Tao of Writing". Adams Media. Avon, Massachusetts. 210pp.

Willliamson, Marianne. 1996. "A Return to Love: Reflections on the Principles of A Course in Miracles". Harper Paperbacks. 336pp.

Chapter 4: HOW TO KEEP GOING

Every blade of grass has its Angel that bends over it and whispers, 'Grow, grow'—The Talmud

4.1 How to Keep Going When You Really Don't Want To

Go confidently in the direction of your dreams! Live the life you've imagined—Henry David Thoreau

There will come a time when you just don't feel like writing in your journal, when you are blue or frustrated or angry, even. It may be that you're just bored with your journal, with your work and school and life in general. It may be simply that you have nothing to say, your muses have fled to Tahiti or someplace far away and you are left with a blank page or more importantly—and alarmingly—a blank mind.

■ Chasing the Journeying Muse

Here's my solution: don't sweat it. Embrace the emptiness and something wonderful will fill it. I said *something*; not necessarily what you expect. I believe that when your muse "leaves" you, it is on a journey. More to the point *you* are on a journey. You're living. More often than not, our directed muse leaves us because something has gotten in the way. What you probably need to do is pay attention to that something. It's telling you something. Ironically, by doing this, you open yourself to something wonderful. Okay, enough of somethings!...

Writing is a lot like fishing. In order to write you need something to write about. So, when the world gets in your way, you should pay attention. This is what you're here for. A writer is an artist who reports on her society. A good artist, at least an accessible one, needs to be both participant as well as observer. So, take a break and live. Chances are, you will have much more to write about after you do.

■ Dealing with Writer's Block

I'm not a very patient person. I make no time for writer's block or lingering in useless limbo over some plot issue or misbehaving minor character. I write pretty much to a tight schedule: this short story to that market by this date; edits to this book to the editor by that date; blog posts created by such and such a time; an article to another market by another date. It goes on and on. When I go to my computer to write, I *write*.

Then there's Sammy. My cat.

Who likes to jump on my lap, make himself all comfortable and then lie over my arm—trapping it along with five of my typing digits. Now what??? Some of you would advise me to simply pull out my pinned arm and/or shove him off. But how can I disturb such a blissful creature? He is so content furled on me, so satisfied that he has captured that wandering appendage of business that is all his now. Content in the bliss of now.

Pinned in the moment, my mind first struggles with the need to pound out the next line. My mind then rephrases and teases out nuances of that line. Finally, it wanders out with my gaze and I find myself day-dreaming in a kind of trance. It is here that magic happens. In the being; not in the doing.

This is the irony of writing and the muse. To write we need to live; we need to have something to write about and we need to be in that state of mind that allows us to set it to print. I am at my best as a writer when I am focused on the essence of the story, its heart and soul beating through me with a life of its own.

My cat Sammy isn't the only vehicle to my magical muses.

—Waking Up The Muse

Here are a few things that help me entice those capricious muses into action:

Music: music moves me in inexplicable ways. I use music to inspire my "muse". Every book I write has its thematic music, which I play while I write and when I drive to and from work (where I do my best plot/theme thinking). I even go so far as to have a musical theme for each character. You can do the same for your journals.

Walks: going for a walk, particularly in a natural environment, uncluttered with human-made distractions, also opens the mind and soul. It grounds you back to the simplicity of life, a good place to start.

Cycling: one of my favorite ways to clear my

mind is to cycle (I think any form of exercise would suffice); just getting your heart rate up and pumping those endorphins through you soothes the soul and unleashes the brain to freely run the field.

Attend literary functions: go to the library and listen to a writer read from her work. You never know how it might inspire you. Browse the book-shelves of the library or bookstore. Attend a writer's convention or conference.

Visit an art gallery, go to a movie: art of any kind can inspire creativity. Fine art is open to interpretation and can provoke your mind in ways you hadn't thought before. If you go with an appreciative friend and discuss what you've seen you add another element to the experience.

Go on a trip with a friend: tour the city or, better yet, take a road trip with a good friend or alone (if you are comfortable with it). I find that travelling is a great way to help me focus outward, forget myself, and open my mind and soul to adventure and learning something new. Road trips are metaphoric journeys of the soul.

Form a writer's or journal-keeping group: sharing ideas with people of like mind (or not, but of respectful mind) can both inspire you and provide the seeds of ideas.

4.2 Invite Creativity to Scintillate Through You—Tap Your Artistic Reservoir

Creativity is harnessing universality and making it flow through your eyes—Peter Koestenbaum

"Creativity is God's gift to us," says Julia Cameron, author of *The Artist's Way.* "Using our creativity is our gift back to God."

Brenda Ueland answers the question of why we should all use our creative power: "Because there is nothing that makes people so generous, joyful, lively, bold and compassionate, so indifferent to fighting and the accumulation of objects and money."

■ Stoke the Artist Inside You

"Many of us wish we were more creative," Cameron shares. "Many of us sense we are more creative, but unable to effectively tap that creativity. Our dreams elude us. Our lives feel somehow flat. Often, we have great ideas, wonderful dreams, but are unable to actualize them for ourselves. Sometimes we have specific creative longings we would love to be able to fulfill...we hunger for what might be called creative living."

Many of us are, in fact, creatively blocked (this is not unlike writer's block, which I discuss above). How would you know if you were? Jealousy is an excellent clue, says Cameron. Are there creative people you resent? Do you tell yourself, 'I could do that, if only...' An old friend of mine used to constantly share that he would "start living and settle down" once he had enough money. It never happened; and he never did—twenty years later. That was sad; because he was waiting for life to begin, when it was already happening—and he was missing it.

Creative recovery (or discovery) is something you can learn. It is something you can enhance and direct. "As you learn to recognize, nurture, and protect your inner artist," says Cameron, 'you will be able to move beyond pain and creative constriction. You will learn ways to recognize and resolve fear, remove emotional scar tissue, and strengthen your confidence."

—Stoke Your Brain

Stoking the creative artist inside you may be as simple as giving your mind the chance to wander—and taking the time to pay attention. Cameron talks about how "rhythm" and regular, repetitive actions play a role in priming the artistic well. She lightheartedly describes how the "s" activities work so well for this: showering, swimming, scrubbing, shaving, steering a car. I can testify to the latter—how many great plot ideas have I cooked up while driving to work! Filmmaker Steven Spielberg claimed that his best ideas came to him while he was driving the freeway. Negotiating through the flow of traffic triggered the artist-brain with images, translated into ideas. "Why do I get my best ideas in the shower?" Einstein was known to have remarked. Scientists tell us that this is because showering is an artist-brain activity.

The magic part in this is to pay attention. Pay attention to your life experiences; don't ignore them. Sit up in the bus and watch people, play with the images, sounds and smells. Get sensual and let your eyes, ears, nose and limbs delight in the world. It's amazing how interesting the world becomes once you start paying attention.

—"Morning Pages"

One tool for creative recovery and discovery is Julia Cameron's "Morning Pages", described in her book *The Artist's Way*. Essentially an exercise in stream-of-conscious writing—she prescribes three pages of longhand every morning just after you rise—the "Morning Pages" or their equivalent can lead to "a connection with a source of wisdom within". I talk about it some more below, in Section 4.5.

4.3 Relax and Have Fun

What we play is life—Louis Armstrong

■ Get Comfortable with Something Familiar

I found in my daily writing that I had developed a comfortable routine that helped me to relax before I began. The time wasn't necessarily the same when I sat down to write, but the routine of getting ready was: after supper and a good visit with my husband and son, I settled at my large oak roll top desk with a cup of hot tea, a lit candle and the cat at my feet; those were my mantra for writing. It was like a "sacred ceremony" to prepare and honor my muse. I talk more about creating a routine and how it can help you write in Section 4.6.

111

■ Tools to Relax

There's no point in even thinking you are going to write if you are too upset, agitated or in a rage. It's better to do something physical; go for a run, take a long walk, or visit the gym and play a sport or work out. Visit with a good friend. Browse the Internet for information, watch a show or play a computer game.

Try stretching, yoga or meditation to help you relax. Playing a piece of music you enjoy can help you relax and invoke the muse at the same time (more on that below!).

4.4 Find Your Sense of Humor & Practice Gratitude

We can only be said to be alive in those moments when our hearts are conscious of our treasures—Thornton Wilder

Celebrate the humor in things. Learn to laugh at yourself and with others. Write about what you are grateful for.

■ Cultivate Gratitude

At the root of good humor lies gratitude and a secure self-identity.

"A thankful person is thankful under all circumstances," says Bahaullah, founder of the Bahai faith. It was Lao Tse who said that if you rejoice in the

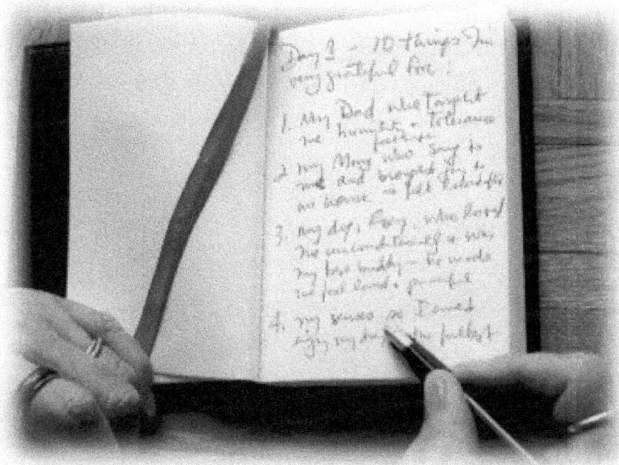

way things are, the whole world will belong to you. Professor and poet Johannes A. Gaertner eloquently said: "To speak gratitude is courteous and pleasant, to enact gratitude is generous and noble, but to live gratitude is to touch Heaven."

In her book *The Magic*, Rhonda Byrne shares how cultivating gratitude in all aspects of your life can empower you and provide you with a healthy joyful life. "Gratitude is magnetic," says Byrne. "The more gratitude you have the more abundance you magnetize." You can tell how much you have actually used gratitude in your life, says Byrne: "just take a look at all of the major areas in your life: money, health, happiness, career, home, and relationships. The areas of

113

your life that are abundant and wonderful are where you have used gratitude and are experiencing the magic as a result. Any areas that are not abundant and wonderful are due to a lack of gratitude." Whenever something or someone is taken for granted, it is not surprising that they often end up taking flight. The bottom line of ungratefulness, says Byrne is that "when we're not grateful, *we're taking*; we're taking things in our life for granted. When we take things for granted we are unintentionally taking from ourselves." To receive you have to give. And giving thanks is one of the most powerful ways of giving.

Let us rise up and be thankful, for if we didn't learn a lot today, at least we learned a little, and if we didn't learn a little, at least we didn't get sick, and if we got sick, at least we didn't die, so let us all be thankful—Gautama Buddha

—Count Your Blessings

"Intentions, compressed into words enfold magical power," medical doctor and writer Deepak Chopra tells us. There is an ancient mantra that goes something like this: *where you place your attention, there you are.* It speaks to the ultimate power of intent. When intention and feeling gratitude come together, you get magic, real magic.

Byrne prescribes a daily exercise that will help you begin your day with a healthy and happy attitude. It starts with literally counting your blessings. Here's how it works:

1. First thing in the morning, make a list of TEN blessings in your life that you are grateful for. It

could be anything from the birds singing in your back yard, the water you are drinking to keep you alive or your eyes to see the trees or ears to hear the birds to your parents who provided for you.

2. Write why you are grateful for each blessing. Give at least one reason.

3. Go back and read your list, either in your mind or out loud. When you get to the end of each one, say the words *thank you, thank you, thank you*, and feel the gratitude for that blessing as much as you possibly can.

4. Repeat the first three steps of this magical practice every morning for the next 27 days.

Better to lose count while naming your blessings than to lose your blessings to counting your troubles—Maltbie D. Babcock

■ Cultivate Humor & Happiness

Cultivating your sense of humor doesn't mean that you need to start learning how to tell jokes. Far from it. It means cultivating an attitude in life where you recognize the irony and humor in your surroundings. Try to see the humor in situations, particularly those that make you angry. It's always there; it just takes a bit of effort to see it. And by looking for it, you are helping your own mind gain a better and healthier perspective on the whole situation.

You'll find that you have your own particular sense of humor, based on your own history, background and philosophies. Because of this, some things will be funny to you and not others. Discover your humor and cultivate it. Practice smiling and laughing daily. Part of cultivating your humor is knowing what is funny to you. Ways to do this include:

- watching humorous shows, movies and TV shows
- reading humorous books and stories that see the lighter side of things
- hanging out with fun and funny people (their humor rubs off!)

HelpGuide.org provides some ways that you can bring more humor and laughter into your life:

- **Smile:** Smiling is the beginning of laughter. Like laughter, it's contagious. Pioneers in "laugh therapy," find it's possible to laugh without even experiencing a funny event. The same holds for smiling. When you look at someone or see something even mildly pleasing, practice smiling.

- **Count your blessings:** Literally make a list. The simple act of considering the good things in your life will distance you from negative thoughts that are a barrier to humor and laughter. When you're in a state of sadness, you have further to travel to get to humor and laughter.

- **When you hear laughter, move toward it:** Sometimes humor and laughter are private, a shared joke among a small group, but usually not. More often, people are very happy to share something funny because it gives them an opportunity to laugh again and feed off the humor you find in it. When you hear laughter, seek it out and ask, "What's funny?"

- **Spend time with fun, playful people:** These are people who laugh easily—both at themselves and at life's absurdities—and who routinely find the humor in everyday events. Their playful point of view and laughter are contagious.

- **Bring humor into conversations:** Ask people, "What's the funniest thing that happened to you today? This week? In your life?"

—Ways to Take Yourself Less Seriously

HelpGuide.org gives some excellent ways to help you see the lighter side of life. These include:

- **Laugh at yourself:** Share your embarrassing moments. The best way to take yourself less seriously is to talk about times when you took yourself too seriously.

- **Attempt to laugh at situations rather than bemoan them:** Look for the humor in a bad situation, and uncover the irony and absurdity of life. This will help improve your mood and the mood of those around you.

- **Surround yourself with reminders to lighten up:** Keep a toy on your desk or in your car. Put up a funny poster in your office. Choose a computer screensaver that makes you laugh.

Frame photos of you and your family or friends having fun.

- **Keep things in perspective:** Many things in life are beyond your control—particularly the behavior of other people. While you might think taking the weight of the world on your shoulders is admirable, in the long run it's unrealistic, unproductive, unhealthy, and even egotistical.

- **Deal with your stress:** Stress is a major impediment to humor and laughter.

- **Pay attention to children and emulate them:** They are the experts on playing, taking life lightly, and laughing and finding joy in all things.

4.5 Find Sources of Inspiration

Develop interest in life as you see it; in people, things, literature, music— the world is so rich, simply throbbing with rich treasures, beautiful souls and interesting people. Forget yourself—Henry Miller

Look outward as well as inward and explore different perspectives. Learn something new, find a photo or quote that touches you and write about it. How and why does it affect you? A colleague of mine once said that "there is nothing uninteresting in the world; only disinterested people." Rediscover what interests you. Create interest. Connect with the world. Find beauty.

Who inspires you? Why do they inspire you? What do they inspire *in you*?

Make a list of people (real or fictional, alive or dead) who inspire you and add the reasons why they do. You can take it a step further:

- Research and write a tribute to them
- Create a fantasy in which you meet them and interact with them
- Write a fictional conversation with them or write a letter to them
- Find a quote that epitomizes the essence of that person

Here's mine for a very special mentor, advocate and friend. It's by Albert Schweitzer:

> At times our own light goes out and is rekindled by a spark from another person. Each of us has cause to think with deep gratitude of those who have lighted the flame within us.

Julia Cameron, author of *The Artist's Way*, shares that "art may seem to spring from pain, but perhaps that is because pain serves to focus our attention onto details (for instance, the excruciatingly beautiful curve of a lost lover's neck). Art may seem to involve broad strokes, grand schemes, great plans. But it is the attention to detail that stays with us; the singular image is what haunts us and becomes art. Even in the midst of pain, this singular image brings delight. The artist who tells you different is lying."

Those who don't believe in magic will never find it—Roald Dahl

Artists need to fill their reservoirs. Think magic. Think fun and mystery; not duty. Duty is dull and motionless. A mystery lures you; it keeps you moving

119

and wondering. Do what intrigues you. Explore what interests you. "Think mystery, not mastery," says Cameron.

You can use one of the questions below to prompt the creation of an uplifting dialogue.

- If you were an animal, what would you be and why?
- Name someone dead who you admire; what would you say to them if you could meet them?
- Name five qualities of your best friend.

■ Go on an Artist's Date

In order to write about life, we must *live*. Cameron prescribes an adventure to fill up our artistic reservoir, called an "Artist's Date". This is a block of time that you set aside and commit to; say, for two hours each week. It is a time committed to nurturing your artistic spirit and creativity. It could be an actual excursion, a "play-date" that you plan out and defend against any interlopers, distractions and excuses. This is a gift you give to yourself. You don't take anyone with you. It is a solitary date, a date with yourself. A date with the artist in you. Do something on your own. Go bowling or to a show on your own.

Other examples include:

- A stroll in your neighborhood or in a local park
- A stroll through an interesting ethnic community or funky commercial area
- A trip to the gallery, library, train station, church to people-watch or look at architecture and art, both intentional and otherwise

- A walk on beach to watch the sunset and watch the waves, the pebbles and nature's other artifacts
- A discovery-drive through the country or some place of interest, preferably new to you, and let yourself get lost

"During these periods of relaxation after concentrated intellectual activity, the intuitive mind seems to take over and can produce the sudden clarifying insights which give so much joy and delight," says physicist Fritjog Capra.

■ "Morning Pages"—or "Garbage Out"

In Chapter 3, I mentioned Julia Cameron's "Morning Pages" as a technique to get you started.

Cameron describes how her program of stream-of-consciousness longhand writing every morning also helped a friend find inspiration. Here's how she described it: "Phyllis, a leggy, racehorse socialite who for years had hidden her brains behind her beauty and her life behind her man's, tried the morning pages with a great deal of surface cheer—and an inner conviction they would never work for her. It had been years since she had allowed herself to write anything other than letters and bread-and-butter lists. About a month into the morning pages, seemingly out of nowhere, Phyllis got her first poem." Three years later she had written poems, speeches, radio shows, and a non-fiction book.

"Although occasionally colorful, the morning pages are often negative, frequently fragmented, often self-pitying, repetitive, stilted or babyish, angry or bland—even silly sounding. Good!" says Cameron, who adds that all that "garbage" stands between you and your creative inspiration. Getting the garbage out can clear the mind.

Morning Pages are not meant to be great literature; they're not meant to be anything, actually. Their role is simply to "get to the other side"; the other side of our fear and censors, of our negativity and miserable moods. They are not meant to be read, kept or reflected upon. They are a vehicle to rid you of the garbage inside, to free your mind to move on to the good stuff. Morning Pages provide the role of "therapeutic writing" I mentioned in Chapter 2.

4.6 Create a Routine & Fun Association

The position of the artist is humble. He is essentially a channel—Piet Mondrian

In Chapter 2, I discuss the importance for you to find a time and place to write that works for you. Finding both the right place and time to write is giving yourself the gift of enablement. There is no point in deciding to keep a journal if you don't have the time to write one—or more to the point if you don't choose a realistic time and place that will enable you to write. So, keeping your commitment to write by choosing the best time and place to do it, is important.

Creating a routine helps a lot. Routines turn into habits and habits become part of unconscious behavior.

Here are a few tips to help keep you writing:

• Make sure you choose a time that is right for the kind of writing you're doing

- Choose a place that lets you think freely and without distraction and interruption and where you feel safe

- Evaluate your choices from time to time to optimize your writing; you may need to change your location or time as things change around you

- Create a routine that works within your daily schedules and inclinations to settle into a self-fulfilling habit

- Adopt a pleasant habit that you can look forward to and which you can associate with writing your journal. In Section 4.2 I told you about my habit of making a hot tea and lighting a candle before starting. If you associate writing in your journal with an activity you enjoy, you are more likely to write. Find something that you can link to journal writing.

■ What To Do About Skipping & Gaps in Journaling

Don't fret about it. When you skip a period of no writing, don't feel compelled to fill in the time you missed with the same detailed writing prior to your hiatus. Simply summarize that time in accordance with your feelings and what happened. Then continue on. Many journal writers who have journals spanning many years may have large gaps between meaningful entries that pick up from where they left off.

Here's a great philosophy that blogger Cory wisely shared about skipping:

> I often find myself in a frenzy if I haven't written anything in a while in my journal. When I start writing again, I feel this overwhelming urge to "update" my journal about EVERY LITTLE THING that has happened since I last wrote. _Resist that urge if at all possible!_

> I have heard from several people who keep journals that your "blank spots" in your journal have just as big a story to tell as your daily entries do. Maybe, like me, you were in the hospital. Maybe someone else was in the hospital. Maybe, heaven forbid, your laptop got stolen. Maybe it was just a time in the year at your place of employment where you were incredibly busy.

> It's OK not to write in your journal from time to time. It's ALSO OK to resist the urge to not chronicle those lost days, weeks or months with a minute-by-minute or day-by-day

recap of events. By all means, if you want to write in your journal about what kept you from writing for an extended length of time, write about it. Just don't get caught up in the minute details...I find that that obsession with wanting to recap every little thing gets in the way of beginning your writing again...then you just don't want to write...By all means SUMMARIZE things that have happened since you last wrote.

4.7 Change It Up—Diversify & Intensify

The purpose of art is not a rarified, intellectual distillate— it is life, intensified, brilliant life— Alain Arias-Misson

Someone once said that "a change is as good as a rest". This truism applies equally to journal-writing. If you find yourself in a rut of dutiful routine or mundane, change it up. Here's an example scenario:

You are keeping a personal daily journal about your experiences in high school and nothing much is happening that seems new or exciting. You are bored with school and with the journal. The text reads like a flat pancake, and not a very tasty one at that.

Here are a few things you can do:

- Google an inspirational quote and write about it (it could even be about "boredom"; you'd be surprised what neat stuff is out there!)

- Give your journal a face-lift by adding pictures or changing its overall design; change your pen or font — that can make a big difference in how and even what you write

- Research a favorite topic and include media clips, links, etc. on it

- Consult a book of wisdom (e.g., the Bible, Talmud or Koran) or book on mythology or folktales; pick a passage and write how it relates to you

- Stop writing about your day and use other ways to express your feelings; examples include drawing and doodling, using pictures, quotes, or YouTube videos

- Give that journal a hiatus and start a new journal on some favorite theme or in a new platform (e.g., if you were using the computer, create a journal on paper or vice versa; start a themed journal if you were keeping a daily personal journal)

4.8 Use the Journal to Work Through the Hard Stuff

It always comes back to the same necessity: go deep enough and there is a bedrock of truth, however hard— May Sarton

Many researchers, psychotherapists and psychiatrists believe that mental illness and suicidal despair are not caused so much by the trauma itself, but because the survivor can't verbalize what's happened and what they have suffered: because they weren't "able to describe their feelings of rage, anger, humiliation, despair, helplessness, and sadness," says psychotherapist Alice Miller. Feeling despair, contends DeSalvo, suggests that there's a story that hasn't been told and that feelings linked to the story have not been expressed, particularly—I would add—to an appreciative and compassionate ear.

Left unexpressed, the effects of trauma can become toxic.

▪ Writing That Heals

DeSalvo tells us that "writing that describes traumatic or distressing events in detail and how we felt about these events then and now is the only kind of writing about trauma that clinically has been associated with improved health."

Simply writing about what you did on a given day or just recording the trauma and venting feelings without linking the two does not result in significant health or emotional benefits, according to Pennebaker and other researchers. In fact, experiments have shown that simply venting feelings can make the writer more sick.

In other words, our health won't improve through free-writing or objective descriptions of our traumas or by simple venting of our emotions. "We cannot simply use writing as catharsis," says DeSalvo. "We must write in a way that *links detailed descriptions of what happened with feelings*—then and now—about what happened." Both thinking and feeling are involved and *linking them is critical.*

Pennebaker and his associates showed that only when a writer linked his or her deepest thoughts and feelings to the trauma, did it result in improved immune function and improved emotional and physical health. Benefits occurred regardless of educational level and feedback on what was written.

▪ Transform Yourself from Victim to Survivor

Literary historian Rosaria Champagne, author of *The Politics of Survivorship*, wrote that, "the difference between a survivor of violence and a victim of violence is the political meaning made of the traumatic experience." According to Champagne, a victim complies with the abuse and lets others dismiss it as unimportant. A survivor, on the other hand, rejects the demand to remain politely silent and does not give in to self-effacement.

Survivors may forgive but they don't forget. They speak up and they speak out. Survivors tell stories.

▪ Guidelines for Handling Trauma

After reading Pennebaker's "Opening Up", DeSalvo created some excellent guidelines for dealing with trauma in your writing.

Do's and Don'ts in Writing About Trauma

Do's ...

Write twenty minutes a day over a period of four days. Do this periodically. This way you won't feel overwhelmed.

Write in a private, safe, comfortable environment.

Write about issues you're currently living with, something you're thinking or dreaming about constantly, a trauma you've never disclosed or discussed or resolved.

Write about joys and pleasures too.

Write about what happened. Write, too, about feelings about what happened. What do you feel? Why do you feel this way? Link events with feelings.

Try to write an extremely detailed, organized, coherent, vivid, emotionally compelling narrative. Don't worry about correctness, about grammar or punctuation.

Beneficial effects will occur even if no one reads your writing. If you choose to keep your writing and not discard it, you must safeguard it.

Expect, initially, that in writing this way you will have complex and appropriately difficult feelings. Make sure you get support if you need it.

Don'ts ...

Don't use writing as a substitute for taking action.

Don't become overly intellectual.

Don't use writing as a way of complaining. Use it, instead, to discover how and why you feel as you do. Simply complaining or venting will probably make you feel worse.

Don't use your writing to become overly self-absorbed. Over-analyzing everything is counterproductive.

Don't use writing as a substitute for therapy or medical care.

Reference: DeSalvo, 2000.

Exploring your feelings is a key element in writing about trauma. Sometimes you don't know how or why you feel the way you do...writing about it can help you discover not only what you feel but why you feel this way. To help you describe, pay attention to your verbs; keep them active (e.g., "I enjoyed the pie" instead of "the food was good"). DeSalvo's "Don'ts" are critical to keeping a healthy attitude. You undermine the benefit of expression if you apply it obsessively and stay only in the negative. Learn to step away and balance reporting with reflection and action. See Section 4.9 on storytelling for more strategies on writing that can help heal trauma.

■ Try It Yourself...

You might want to try the exercise below to get a feel for meaningful expressive writing. It is an evolving process of learning by doing. In other words, you get better at it as you go along. Don't let the process intimidate you. Just keep going and it will get easier.

Exercise:

For the next 4 days, spend about 15 minutes to write your very deepest thoughts and feelings about the most traumatic experience of your entire life or an extremely important emotional issue that has affected you and your life.

You may wish to tie your topic to your relationships with others, like parents, sweethearts, friends or relatives; to your past, present or future; or to who you have been, would like to be or are right now. You may stick with the same topic and expand it over the four days or write about different topics each day. This is just for your eyes. It's totally up to you whether you share this with anyone.

Don't worry about spelling or grammar or sentence structure. The only rule is that once you begin writing you continue until the 15 minutes is over.

Some Suggestions:

- Find a best time and place to write and follow the suggestions on journaling in Chapters 4 through 7; don't write a bedtime.

- Write by hand or on computer

- Play soft music while writing

- Answer a set of questions you pose

- Don't worry about grammar and structure

- Think about a topic prior to the session

Reference: DeSalvo, 2000.

CAUTIONARY NOTE: If you are suffering symptoms of post-traumatic stress disorder, writing about severe trauma should be done with professional, qualified, empathic help. Before engaging in any such writing, please get help, get assistance. Make an emergency plan (with qualified assistance) about what you will do if you find you are at extreme risk.

4.9 Write Stories

Imagination is the true magic carpet—Norman Vincent Peale

I'm a storyteller. I shared stories since I was five years old—first with my older sister, then with my friends and finally with the world. It was so fun and very fulfilling! Telling fiction stories is a refreshing way to tell our life stories. Whether you choose to write an allegory, folk tale, fantasy or mystery based on your journal entries, this can jumpstart your creativity and give yourself insight as well as cool imaginative ideas.

You can use your journal as source material for compelling fiction. You can even write part of your journal as a fiction story or choose to write your entire journal this way.

■ Fictional Characters and Plot

Inventing what our fictional characters feel and think helps us understand ourselves and overcome difficulties. I talk more about writing stories not just to keep going but to get the most out of our journals in Chapter 5.

Choosing to tell parts of "your story" through fiction stories can be one of the most fulfilling aspects of journaling. This form of writing can get you writing again if you're stuck. Think of the possibilities, and the wealth of awesome characters you can draw from: villains, heroes, lovers and mentors (e.g., the bully in school, the teacher you have a crush on, your unfeeling boss). Or plots and emotional issues: love, betrayal, fear, intrigue, lies, cheating, jealousy, redemption and altruism. Storytelling can help you keep going during a difficult time, when writing directly and honestly about something or someone is too raw, too difficult.

Use metaphor, personification and allegory to help you get past that sticky place. You may choose to write a portion or your entire journal through "story" and fictionalized characters. See Chapter 5 for more on storytelling.

—Using Metaphor

Metaphors directly compare seemingly unrelated subjects as being similar or equal to each other (e.g., in the expression "love danced in her heart" love is compared to a dancer). We use metaphor all the time in casual language: "It's raining cats and dogs", "his old flame", "the table leg" "fishing for information".

Because metaphor uses one thing to represent another, it is a powerful vehicle for conveying information that seems beyond the limits of language. Metaphors can really help a person who may find it difficult to describe an experience directly; it encourages interpretation by describing an indirect rather than a literal truth (e.g., "the darkness embraced her"). Metaphor compacts meaning but also evokes emotion, letting us express uniquely as individuals. An example of giving maximum meaning with a minimum of words is: "John's office was a prison". This simple four-word comparison of an office to a prison creates rich and complex images and impressions of John's office and— more importantly—how John felt about the office. Metaphors create new meanings through writing about personal feelings and experiences.

133

—Personification

Personification gives an idea, object, or animal the qualities of a person (e.g., a babbling brook; the darkness embraced her).

—Allegories

Allegories equate an object, person or action with a meaning that lies outside the narrative. Allegory has both a literal and a representative meaning. Allegories can describe political or historic events and people or they can represent ideas. George Orwell's *Animal Farm* is a good example. *Animal Farm* makes commentary on the development of communism in Russia through a revolt by farm animals. Dante's *Divine Comedy* is another example of an allegory, in which the pilgrim Dante, representing the Common Person, seeks salvation and is both helped and hindered by his reliance on Reason, in the person of Virgil.

Think of the interesting allegories you can write, starring characters and a world that personifies thoughts, people, and ideas from your personal world. For instance, that bully in school could become drug dealer "Bert Totenkopf" in your urban fantasy, in which you are Gaia, a superhero. You could write your entire journal this way—in "code"—which would serve several purposes including that of "safety". Refer to Chapter 5, Section 5.3, for more tools you can use for writing allegories. Chapter 6 gives you more tools on the safety side of storytelling.

—Myths & Your "Hero's Journey"

Myths are stories we tell each other about what it means to be human. The ancient myths are woven into the very fabric of our modern world. They are part of our daily lives and culture and form the basis of many of our stories: hero's quests, father-son conflicts, and the struggle to create a just society. Visiting your stories through the lens of mythology and the archetypes of the hero's journey concept can help you work through things and keep going. I talk more about The Hero's Journey in storytelling in Chapter 5.

"Most of us are slaves of the stories we unconsciously tell ourselves about our lives," Carol S. Pearson, author of *The Hero Within: Six Archetypes We Live By*, tells us. "Freedom begins the moment we become conscious of the plot line we are living and, with this insight, recognize that we can step into another story altogether." When you explore the archetypes of your own story, you may be surprised at what you discover. You may achieve new clarity that will help you continue in your journal journey as well.

—Recognizing Archetypes

Psychologist Carl Jung tells us that archetypes are irrepressible, unconscious, pre-existing forms of the psyche shared by cultures and societies through common symbols and images.

Archetypes can be viewed as inner potentialities or guides that preside in your heroic journey: the journey of finding and expressing your true self in a way that makes a genuine contribution to the world.

Pearson describes six major archetypal perspectives that read like a central character in a movie, each with their own plot.

Six Archetypes We Live By

Archetype	Task	Gift
Orphan	Survive difficulty	Resilience
Wanderer	Find yourself	Independence
Warrior	Prove your worth	Courage
Altruist	Show generosity	Compassion
Innocent	Achieve happiness	Faith
Magician	Transform your life	Power

Reference: Pearson, 1998.

To discover which archetypal plot dominates your life, pay attention to your conversation. What stories are you weaving about yourself?

Let's take the example of you going for a job interview and not getting the job:

- **Orphan:** "It was unfair. I was the most qualified candidate. You just can't win."

- **Wanderer:** "Soon after I got there I realized I wouldn't like it there. It seemed so confining. I could hardly wait to escape."

- **Warrior:** "I was definitely the best qualified candidate. I'm going to convince them to hire me."

- **Altruist:** "I felt really happy for the person who got the job."

- **Innocent:** "I'm sure the right job for me will be there at the right time."

- **Magician:** "I didn't get the job, but I learned something very important about landing the position that really is right for me."

How you tell the stories about your life reflects your self-image and predicts how much or how little you expect in the future.

—Stories We Must Tell

In her book *Mathilda*, Mary Shelley (author of *Frankenstein*) wrote about a character who suffered terrible abuse and loss, like Mary did. With no support from her stern family, and on the brink of suicide, Mary turned to her writing and created a suicidal character similar to herself. Mary sacrificed her character and saved herself.

CAUTIONARY NOTE: If you are suffering symptoms of post-traumatic stress disorder, writing about severe trauma should be done with professional, qualified, empathic help. Before engaging in any such writing, please get help, get assistance. Make an emergency plan (with qualified assistance) about what you will do if you find you are at extreme risk.

*Straightaway the ideas flow in upon me, directly from God—*Johannes Brahms

137

4.10 References

Cameron, Julia. 1992. "The Artist's Way". Penguin Putnam Inc., New York, NY. 222pp.

Champagne, Rosaria. 1996. "The Politics of Survivorship." New York University Press. New York, NY.

DeSalvo, Louise. 2000. "Writing as a Way of Healing: How Telling Our Stories Transforms Our Lives." Beacon Press. Boston, MS. 226pp.

Munteanu, Nina. 2009. "The Fiction Writer: Get Published, Write Now!" Starfire World Syndicate. Louisville, KY. 264pp.

Munteanu, Nina. 2010. "The Writer's Toolkit". DVD set. Starfire World Syndicate, Louisville, KY.

O'Brien, Tim. 1990. "The Things They Carried". Houghton Mifflin. New York, NY.

Pearson, Carol S. 1998. "The Hero Within: Six Archetypes We Live By". Harper. San Francisco. 338pp.

Pennebaker, James W., and Sandra Klihr Beall. 1986. "Confronting a Traumatic Event: Toward an Understanding of Inhibition and Disease." *Journal of Abnormal Psychology* 95, no. 3: 274-81.

Ueland, Brenda. 2007. "If You Want to Write: a Book about Art, Independence and Spirit". Graywolf Press.

Chapter 5: HOW TO GET THE MOST OUT OF YOUR JOURNALING

*I paint not by sight but by faith. Faith gives you sight—*Amos Ferguson

5.1 Doing Research

*The appearance of things changes according to the emotions, and thus we see magic and beauty in them, while the magic and beauty are really in ourselves—*Kahlil Gibran

Learn more by researching what you write about. This may provide solutions and ideas to help work out difficulties. It will certainly help to increase your interest and learning in the subject areas you've written about.

Your journal entries may serve the additional purpose of being a resource for something you later wish to investigate. Say, you had made some interesting entries on the cycles of the moon during a particular cosmic occurrence. You may wish to use these observations later in a school project on that cosmic event. Of course, this underscores the merit of keeping an accurate journal when recording natural phenomena, including date and time.

5.2 Harvest Your Journal

He who knows others is wise; he who knows himself is enlightened—Lao-Tse

One of the real benefits of journal writing is the gift of perspective you get from the flow of ideas, experiences and learning through your journal's sustained use over a period of time. The more frequent, detailed and honest your entries have been, the more you will get out of them when you revisit your journal to reflect on what you've written. This is why daily journaling can be so rewarding. Through the lens of perspective over time, you may begin to see patterns in your activities, reactions and observations that you weren't aware of before. It's like Max Planc said about nature: "science cannot solve the ultimate mystery of nature. And that is because, in the last analysis, we ourselves are a part of the mystery that we are trying to solve." When you step out of the stream you were in and look in from outside, you will gain insight through a new perspective. The payoffs can include galvanizing new ideas, arriving at action items that suddenly make sense, and providing material for making new plans.

Make a point of reading your journals. Often. The three steps in harvesting your journal are: 1) read; 2) ponder; and 3) reread. These three steps can be used as many times as you wish. I would add another optional step too: research. During your revisit, you may find a benefit to researching outside your journal for answers or clarification to ideas and concepts and questions that emerge from your review.

Making sense of your journal takes time. Ken Plummer (2001) tells us that this analysis part in the journaling process is the "truly creative part of the work… It entails brooding and reflecting upon mounds of [information] for long periods of time until it makes sense and feels right, and key ideas and themes flow from it. It is also the hardest process to describe." He suggests that the standard technique is to read and make notes (and research), leave and ponder (and research), reread without notes, make new notes, ponder (and research), reread and so on. Ideas and glimmers of understanding emerge. You can deepen these through conversation with others and through research (e.g., reading relevant texts, online searches, etc.).

—What is Truth?

Judith Barrington, author of *Writing the Memoir*, describes factual truth and emotional truth and that they are not necessarily the same thing.

It's important to acknowledge the emotional truth of events and actions in our lives. How you express and remember an event tells you as much about your state of mind and heart then—and now—as the event itself. Understanding the importance of personal truth in capturing the essence of the events as they pertain to you and your life journey can empower you and can also be revealing.

■ Questions To Ask as You Review Your Journal

Here are some basic questions you can ask yourself as you reread your journal:

- Do any experiences, situations or understandings stand out for you? What is it about them that is catching your attention?

- Does what you have written in your journal still resonate with you? Were you fully honest and do the interpretations you made at the time still make sense? From your present standpoint and understanding, are there items you need to re-interpret?

- Is there anything missing? Was there something revealed that you evaded?

- Can you see any connection with any broader experience, problem or theme you were/are exploring?

You may wish to eventually use your journal(s), whether personal (mixed) or themed, as a research/resource for development of theories or later projects you may embark on—say, a memoir or a project in school or at work that relates to a theme you covered (e.g., on the subject of recycling that you covered in a journal you kept).

■ Making a Themed Index

You may wish to keep the first few pages of

your paper journal free to make an index later that will identify 1) particular aspects touched upon in your journal, 2) themes that have revealed themselves and 3) important milestones recognized in your life story.

Making an index for your journal will help you organize your thoughts and feelings over the time period covered. It will also help you find relevant entries more easily later on.

There are many ways to index and code your journal. It helps if you number the pages first. If you are indexing themes (say, anything to do with your friend Alison)—which you may have made entries about not chronologically but chaotically throughout the journal—you can code any relevant page to Alison with a sticky note of a certain color and refer to that color in your index alongside your reference to "Alison". This way, when you wish to come back and revisit those references to do with Alison specifically, you can simply go to those pages coded with that color.

■ Using Metaphor & Personification

I describe the use of metaphor in Chapter 4. Because metaphor compares one thing to another, when you use metaphor you are linking events or things to your personal feelings, which can reveal, heal and provide directions for action. Because metaphor relies on individual comparison and interpretation, it will mean different things to different people. Let's take the example "the darkness embraced her". When I wrote that line, I was comparing the darkness to a sweetheart. When I shared the metaphor with my writing students, one of them shared that what first came to her mind was an image of a vampire about to devour her. In my

143

mind the darkness was friendly, safe and warmly thrilling; in my student's mind the darkness was sinister, scary and suffocating. What's important is what the metaphor means to *you*. It will help reveal your feelings at the time you wrote.

Exercise:

1. Compare a person you know to the following: a peacock; a sloth; a dung beetle; a rabbit. What physical and emotional connotations do you get?

2. Take a piece of your own writing and find all the metaphors and similes. Highlight them then interrogate them. What do they say?

Reference: Munteanu, 2009

■ Become a "Connoisseur"

Journals are all about expression and learning from it. They enable us to examine ourselves and our world, analyze, conclude and develop. Learning relies on an element of artistry: the ability to improvise, devise new ways of looking at things, and then act on them in new ways. According to Donald Schön (1987) such artistry is an exercise of intelligence—a kind of knowing. Through engaging with our experiences we can develop maxims about, say, working or relating to a group or individual. We learn to appreciate—to be aware and to understand—what we have experienced. "We become connoisseurs." (Eisner, 1998).

According to Eisner (1998) connoisseurship involves the ability to see, not merely to look. This means developing the ability to name and appreciate the different dimensions of situations and experiences, and the way they relate to one another. It means drawing upon and making sense of a wide array of information. It means placing your experiences and understanding in a wider context. And connecting them with your values and commitments. That's where writing and keeping journals comes in.

■ Become a "Critic"

"If connoisseurism is the art of expression, criticism is the art of disclosure" (Eisner, 1998). According to Eisner, the mandate of criticism is the re-education of perception. The task of the critic is to help us see (not just look). In order to learn from what you honestly express, you must don the critic hat and analyze. Think of criticism as the "midwife of perception." It helps perception come into being, then later refines it so you can learn from it.

5.3 Become a Memoirist

Undoubtedly we become what we envisage—Claude M. Bristol

Memoirs are true stories told in the first person about an important aspect of a person's life (e.g., a woman's relationship with her mother, a man's journey through Afghanistan; a woman's experience as a teenager in Egypt). Memoirs can provide a fulfilling venue for expressing your life journey. "Speaking personally and truthfully about our lives [through memoir] plays a small part in erasing years of invisibility and interpretation by others," says memoirist Judith Barrington. "Engaging seriously with

145

the truth challenges our society's enormous untruthfulness—whether it comes from the family, which so often denies its own violence behind closed doors, or from the national and international powers that deny their own violence and call it 'peace keeping'."

When you write a memoir, you legitimize and solidify your truths, your journey and your life. Like any kind of disclosure, there is risk but also incredible fulfillment.

Here are some tips on writing a memoir:

- Write in the first person
- Tell the truth, both emotional and factual
- Express your opinions as opinions and be clear about it
- Focus on a particular theme in your life journey, something that matters
- Tell it like a story that has an ending with resolution (based on the theme)
- Attribute controversial statements to others

5.4 Become a Storyteller

Only when he no longer knows what he is doing does the painter do good things—Edgar Degas

I talk about telling stories in Chapter 4 as one way to drive interest and keep going. Stories are also a wonderful way to explore—usually through metaphor—our experiences with deeper meaning. You can make the most of your experiences in life through interpretive storytelling. I'm not talking about the search for the meaning of life necessarily; I'm talking about *the experience of being alive.*

Joseph Campbell, scholar and mythologist suggests that this is "so that our life experiences on the purely physical plane will have resonances within our own innermost being and reality, so that we actually feel the rapture of being alive."

If you are at all inclined toward fiction writing, try taking source material from your journal— characters, scenes, events—and setting them to "story". This will give you the opportunity to further interpret and explore your feelings and reactions. And have fun doing it! Most literary fiction is, in fact, based on the very real experiences of its authors.

Scholar and mythologist Joseph Campbell tells us that life itself has no meaning—it simply is. It's our stories (pulled out of the ethers of our muse) that give meaning to life. We tell stories about how the world began, our struggles to survive, our victories against greed and evil. At the root of all these lies a universal and timeless human experience. In our stories, meta-phor transcends culture, time and place to help us express our striving journey toward truth, grace and peace.

■ The Power of Myth in Storytelling

"If a being from another world were to ask you, 'How can I learn what it's like to e human?' a good answer would be, 'Study mythology,' " says Campbell. To Campbell, myths express our basic need to explain, celebrate and immortalize the essence of life and our connection to God. The storyteller—whether painter, writer, actor, singer or filmmaker—interprets the divinity in nature for others. We interpret unseen things for a tangible world. Like Dante, we journey to the depths of our world, become its deepest truths to emerge later and share.

▪ The Hero's Journey Myth

I didn't realize when I started writing my adventure stories that I was writing about "the mythic hero's journey"—my hero's journey in its various forms. You can get more out of your journal-writing by applying the Hero's Journey plot approach in storytelling. The Hero's Journey describes a three-stage evolution of every hero, who journeys through "separation", "transformation" and "return".

Stories that pull the reader through the three stages of a hero's journey promise great depth and fulfillment. This kind of storytelling takes us on a transformative journey of learning, self-discovery and self-integration to realize a prevailing victory.

Campbell recognized that myths weren't just abstract theories or quaint ancient beliefs but practical models for understanding how to live. Ultimately, the Hero's Journey is the soul's search for "home". It is a journey we all take in some form. This is why the Hero's Journey model for writing is so relevant and why it appeals to all readers.

Campbell describes a 12-step journey of the hero within 3-acts and influenced by six major archetypes (e.g., herald, mentor, threshold guardian, trickster, shadow and shape-shifter). Our hero starts her journey in Act 1 (the Ordinary World). With the help of herald and mentor, she separates from her known world and enters the Special World in Act 2, where she transforms through her many challenges. In Act 3, she returns to the Ordinary World (no longer ordinary) with her gift to the world. Perhaps the gift is knowledge, or enlightenment or an enabling tool.

The hero archetype is essentially us as we journey to prevail over the obstacles of our fears, weaknesses, and disappointments. Every hero is on a quest or mission, whether she realizes it or not.

■ Using Archetypes in Your Stories

The world of fairy tales and myth is peopled with recurring character types and relationships. Heroes on a quest; heralds and wise old men or women who provide them with "gifts" or motive; shady fellow-travelers—threshold guardians—who "block" the quest; tricksters, who confuse things; and evil villains who simply want to destroy our hero and her quest.

Archetypes refer to ancient patterns of personality shared by humanity. They model a personality or behavior. For instance, a mother figure is an archetype. Archetypes are found in nearly all forms of literature, with their motifs mostly rooted in folklore.

Assigning an archetype to a character lets the writer clarify that character's role in the story. Archetypes are an important tool in the universal language of storytelling, just as myth serves the overall purpose of supplying "the symbols that carry the human spirit forward," Campbell tells us.

Christopher Vogler, author of *The Writer's Journey*, lists the seven most useful archetypes for the writer.

—The Hero

The hero goes on a quest and sacrifices her own needs on behalf of others. She provides a character for us to identify with and is usually the principal character. The hero transforms through her journey as she encounters other archetypes on her journey.

—The Mentor

The mentor often possesses divine wisdom and has faith in the hero. He often gives the hero a "gift", which is usually something important for the quest; either a weapon to destroy a "monster" or a "talisman" to enlighten the hero. A good example is in Star Wars, when Luke's mentor, Obi Wan, provides him with his father's light saber (Luke's magic talisman).

—The Herald

Heralds announce the coming of significant change, whether the hero likes it or not (and usually they don't). Heralds deliver the call to adventure. The herald is a catalyst that enters the story and makes it impossible for the hero to remain in the Ordinary World. Existing in the form of a person, an event, or a message, they shift the hero's balance and change our hero's world.

—The Threshold Guardian

This archetype guards the threshold of

separation from the Ordinary World on the hero's quest to achieve his destiny. Threshold guardians spice up the story by providing obstacles the hero must over-come. Threshold guardians are not usually the main antagonist. They can even be a friend who doesn't believe in the hero or her quest.

—The Shape-shifter

The shape-shifter adds dramatic tension to the story and provides the hero with a puzzle to solve. They can seem one thing and in fact be another. They bring doubt and suspense to the story and test the hero's abilities to discern her path.

— The Shadow

The monster under the bed, repressed feelings, deep trauma, a festering guilt: these all possess the dark energy of the shadow. The shadow archetype is the dark force of the unexpressed, unrealized, rejected, feared aspects of the hero and represented by the main antagonist or villain.

—The Trickster

Practically every Shakespearian play contains a jester or fool, who not only serves as comic relief but as commentator. This is because tricksters are usually witty and clever, even when ridiculous. The comedy of most successful comedians touches upon the pulse of a culture by offering commentary that is truism and often in the form of entertaining sarcasm.

■ Allegories

In Chapter 4, I talked about using allegories as one way to express yourself and to help you keep going. Because allegories have both a literal and a representative meaning, you can adopt them to your own life story and have fun as you learn more about yourself and others in doing it. Allegories are one form of Hero's Journey, often drawing on myth and fairy tale, and clearly making use of archetypes.

Think of the interesting allegories you could write, starring characters and a world that personifies thoughts, people, and ideas from your personal world. You can have lots of fun while achieving depth through symbolism.

Every aspect of your allegory represents something. Names are particularly important and can often be very obvious in this way (e.g., Sir Good the Knight). The name "John" suggests the common man, "Mary" suggests a mother-figure, and the nickname "Red" suggests passion or anger. Pick your names carefully and have fun with them.

For instance, your tyrannous teacher may become the evil and charismatic Prince Sinestra in your epic fantasy or the conniving John Shadow in your detective story. Your favorite aunt could be your hero's trusted mentor, Gaia, in your adventure story. Your untrustworthy and unreliable "shape-shifting" friend could become the frustrating Nick Malatesta ("headache" in Italian).

If you're interested in writing and publishing fiction, check out our companion guidebook *The Fiction Writer: Get Published, Write Now!* It provides you with basic and easy to learn tools for getting started.

5.5 References

Barrington, Judith. 2002. "Writing the Memoir". The Eighth Mountain Press. Portland, OR. 187pp.

Campbell, Joseph. 1988. "The Power of Myth: with Bill Moyers". MJF Books. New York, NY. 293pp.

Eisner, Elliot W. 1998. "The art of educational evaluation: a personal view." Falmer Press. London.

Munteanu, Nina. 2009. "The Fiction Writer: Get Published, Write Now!" Starfire World Syndicate. Louisville, KY. 264pp.

Plummer, Ken. 2001. "Documents of Life 2: an invitation to a critical humanism." Sage. London.

Schőn, Donald. 1987. "The Reflective Practitioner. How professionals think in action." Temple Smith. London.

Vogler, Christopher. 1998. "The Writer's Journey: Mythic Structure for Writers". 2nd Edition. Michael Wiese Productions, Studio City, California. 326pp.

Chapter 6: KEEP YOUR JOURNAL SAFE

Safety doesn't happen by accident—Anonymous

Safety is an important topic from several viewpoints. It's important for you to feel safe and be safe in your journaling. This includes maintaining privacy, autonomy, security and integrity. It also means being secure in the material you've created and in the tools you use (e.g., computer, notebook).

6.1 Keeping Your Journal Private

He that respects himself is safe from others; he wears a coat of mail that none can pierce—Henry Wadsworth Longfellow

■ Paper Journals

There are two ways to maintain privacy. One is to announce your security in an open declaration of journal keeping and the other is through secrecy. Which way you go will determine the measures you need to take to maintain a secure journal that no one will pry into, vandalize or abuse.

—Open Approach

Let's start with the open approach. This really depends on three things: 1) the kind of person you are; 2) the kind of journal you're keeping; and 3) your relationship with your community. For instance, you may decide to keep an open Nature Journal in which you share musings and poetry on Nature and the environment; but wish to keep your personal journal more private. Keeping an open policy allows you to walk anywhere with your journal and not have to hide it, disguise it or lie about it. Because everyone will know you are keeping a journal, you will have both the freedom to write anywhere (because you are openly carrying it everywhere) and run the risk of disclosure or vandalism everywhere. If you decide to keep a journal openly, here are some things you may wish to do:

- use a journal that locks; you can either wear your key openly around your neck like a necklace, which will show everyone that your journal locks and discourage them from trying to look at it, or keep the key hidden in a less obtrusive approach.

- Make a point of keeping everything in your journal palatable for the public; in other words, when you write in it, write for "the world", then it won't matter if someone reads it.

- Alternatively, you could write "in code" or fictionalize places and people through "story". Keep your lexicon or legend separate from the journal itself so that prying eyes won't be able to make the connection.

- Don't advertise that you are keeping a journal; most won't bother if you don't make it look enticing.

- don't act smug or particularly protective with your journal; you're asking for trouble from the worst trouble-makers if you do.

—Secret Approach

Keeping your journal a secret will certainly prevent people from trying to read it. What they don't know is there won't make them curious. However, this is only as good as your efforts in secrecy. Often the very act of keeping a secret creates intrigue, which is extremely delicious to some people—the wrong people, in most cases. So, by keeping your journal a secret, you may be inadvertently inviting interest from the worst people. Keep this in mind as you embark on your secret.

Here are some things you can do to successfully keep your journal a secret:

- If you are taking your journal with you, don't tell anyone it's a journal or diary. If someone asks you about it, particularly if it's locked, tell them that it contains science notes and you didn't have any other notebook to write in.

- Cultivate a nonchalant attitude. If you are anxious or openly secretive or protective, this will attract their interest and curiosity.

- Write in another language or in a secret code. Keep the legend for your code in another secure place.

- Fill the first pages with innocuous material, say math or science or shopping lists. This may help confuse those who give it a cursory glance.

- Write in the third person (to mimic a story) or indeed write your journal as a story.

- Disguise your journal by using boring looking paper (e.g., loose leaf in a binder) or an old beat-up notebook.

- Keep your journal at home and write in the safety and privacy of your room or other safe place away from prying eyes. Confine your artistic sketching and doodling to this environment. You have the option of using a mobile device (e.g., tablet, iPad, etc.) with or without a journal-writing app, to make your field entries and then transfer your notes in your journal at home. Using a mobile device is less curious, given that most people are using them for other forms of communication.

- Consider using a voice activated or pin code mobile device like a notebook, iPad, etc. that you can then download onto your main computer with journal.

- Find good hiding spots. Be creative. Hiding your journal among other books works well. You can go a step further by using a boring book jacket of another book and putting it on your journal. Another good spot is in among your clothes, say your underwear. A fellow journaler suggested hiding your journal in a clean trash can and put the trash bag in, over your diary with a bit of garbage. Another great hiding spot is between the back of a framed picture and the wall.

- Make a decoy journal that you leave out for snoops to read. Add bogus entries ever so often with what the snooper will recognize as fantasy (e.g., your trip to the moon or your years spent in an orphanage). This may confuse them about what is real and what is fantasy, particularly if you tell them you wish to be a fiction writer. The writer Anais Nin did this for years.

- A fellow blogger suggested that reading *Harriet the Spy* by Louise Fitzhugh would help arm you regarding what unkind classmates might do.

■ Computer Journals

Security on your computer is a little easier than with a paper journal you carry around with you. However, there are still ways for people to "break in" and ways for you to ensure security. Here are some tips:

- The obvious first one is to use a dedicated computer with a login, and to use a password encryption to open your word files. You can add more security by naming your folders and files something innocuous (e.g., "English Homework 10" instead of "My Diary").

- Don't use other people's laptops or computers to write your journal. Use one computer dedicated to it; this will help keep "break ins" and leaks to a minimum.

- Download 7-zip, a free utility for Microsoft word or notepad, and you can encrypt (code) your text/photos etc. using 256 bit AES encryption, which is a high security encryption. The Mac-based journal software, Mémoires, uses a password for your journal, and will encrypt it using the industry standard AES-128 cipher.

- Clear your browsing cache. Nosy people can search your browsing cache and find all your good hiding spots.

- Some good hiding places include unlikely file folders with innocuous code names (e.g., iTunes folder, movie-making folders), a jump-drive or memory stick.

6.2 Keeping Your Journal—And Your Information—In Tact

They cannot take away our self-respect if we do not give it to them— Mahatma Gandhi

Aside from the risks to your journal's integrity by journal snatchers, vandals, destroyers and general mischief-makers, there are other ways you can lose your material or have your journal destroyed unin-

tentionally. Whether you are journaling using a paper
notebook, a mobile device or a laptop computer at
home, there are things you can do to ensure the safety
of your precious material. Here are a few tips for all
three kinds:

- Keep your notebook journal in a place where it
  won't get ruined. You may wish to get it copied
  at a copy place and secure the copy in a vault or
  locked chest, etc.

- Maintain back up files (e.g., use a flash drive,
  jump drive or other storage device) and store
  them off your computer in a safe place that
  won't get hot or wet. Back up as often as you
  feel necessary. My benchmark is asking the
  question: how much am I willing to lose?

- Get and use a reliable security system on your
  computer, particularly if you use it a lot to surf
  the Internet. What you need to look for is a
  thorough anti-virus and anti-spyware software
  and a rock-hard firewall. Some of the best Anti-
  Virus Security Programs include: Symantec
  Norton 360; Kaspersky Internet Security; ESET
  NOD32; Avast!; McAfee; and BitDefender.

- Use security software that updates automatically.

- Treat your personal information like cash.

- Secure your wireless network (e.g., use
  encryption in your wireless network and
  router).

- Protect your passwords and don't share them with anyone.

■ Protecting Your Passwords

Here are some tips to help you create strong passwords and keep them safe:

- The longer the password, the tougher it is to crack. Use at least 10 characters; 12 is ideal for most home users.

- Mix letters, numbers, and special characters. Try to be unpredictable—don't use your name, birth date, or common words.

- Don't use the same password for many accounts. If it's stolen from you it can compromise you in many ways and be used to take over those other accounts.

- Don't share passwords on the phone, in texts or by email. No one should ask you for your password. If they do, they are scamming you.

- Keep your passwords in a secure place, out of plain site.

6.3 Online Journaling & Socializing

Better to write for yourself and have no public, than to write for the public and have no self—Cyril Connolly

■ Blogging & Social Networking

—Control Your Privacy

If you enjoy online journaling but aren't ready to expose your innermost thoughts to the world, use a program that lets you turn on privacy. Most reliable social networking sites and online journaling programs provide various levels of privacy. *Penzu* is one example. Penzu is a free, web-based service with an easy-to-use interface. You just sign up for a free account, click the New Entry button, and start typing. You can also upload pictures to your entries on the fly from your computer or a Flickr account. Penzu combines a cool blogging platform with solid privacy features, offering fine-grained control over who sees your writing. Privacy features let you lock down individual posts, or all your entries, depending on your preference. Alternatively, you can email an entry to someone anonymously, or via your Penzu identity.

—What to Share and What Not to Share

Most social networking sites, blogging platforms, and online journaling sites, like Penzu above, provide various levels of privacy that you can select according to your needs. Having said this, there continue to be occurrences of abuse and leaks. No site on the Internet is 100% secure. A word of advice: don't publish anything on the Internet that you don't wish to share with the world.

What about people "stealing" your original stuff? My take on this is that the Internet is pretty much openly public. It is like an open forum of information, data, exchange and sharing. A little like standing in The Piazza San Marco with a bazillion other people, looking, hearing, smelling, touching. It's going to be hard to keep others from taking your stuff and sharing it, in turn, with others. The best way around this is to change your attitude and accept it as the ultimate compliment. When something of yours goes "viral" it's great publicity for you. One thing you can do that most fellow bloggers will respect, is ask to be cited. That way, at least you get the credit for being the originator. This is, in fact, what the Internet does best: SHARE.

—Moderating Comments on Your Blog

You can control the comments that come in on your blog and I highly recommend that you do. You just need to set the moderator on to let you check them before you let them go live. Most blog platforms also have a key (e.g., Captcha) that ensures that a real human is making the comment and keeps span down to a minimum. If you value your blog for its content and style, moderating incoming comments is a great feature. This allows you to "zap" inappropriate remarks using bad or insulting language that will cast a pall over your beautiful blog. They will never see the light of day and not one reader will be exposed to them. It's not cheating. It's just ensuring good manners and keeping your blog clean. There's nothing like one bad comment to stir up more.

Don't let the trolls in.

Bibliography

Algren, Nelson. 1958-1988. In: Plimpton, George (ed.): "Writers at Work". (8 vols). Secker & Warburg. London, UK.

Baikie, Karen & Kay Wilhelm. 2005. "Emotional and physical health benefits of expressive writing." *Advances in Psychiatric Treatment.* 11: 338-346.

Barrington, Judith. 2002. "Writing the Memoir". The Eight Mountain Press, Portland, Oregon. 187pp.

Berry, Wendell. 1990. "What are People For?" North Point Press. San Francisco, CA.

Byrne, Rhonda. 2012. "The Magic". Atria Books. New York, NY.

Cameron, Julia. 1992. "The Artist's Way". Penguin Putnam Inc., New York, NY. 222pp.

Campbell, Joseph. 1988. "The Power of Myth: with Bill Moyers". MJF Books. New York, NY. 293pp.

Champagne, Rosaria. 1996. "The Politics of Survivorship." New York University Press. New York, NY.

Chandler, Daniel. 1987. "Are We Ready for Word-Processors?" *English in Australia* 79: 11-17.

Chandler, Daniel. 1992. "The Phenomenology of Writing by Hand". *Intelligent Tutoring Media* 3(2/3): 65-74.

DeSalvo, Louise. 2000. "Writing as a Way of Healing: How Telling Our Stories Transforms Our Lives." Beacon Press, Boston. 226pp.

Eisner, Elliot W. 1998. "The art of educational evaluation: a personal view." Falmer Press. London.

Goldberg, Natalie. 2005. "Writing Down the Bones: Freeing the Writer Within". Shambhala Publications. Boston, MS. 171pp.

Hieb, Marianne. 2005. "Inner Journeying Through Art-Journaling". Jessica Kingsley Publishers, London, England. 176pp.

Holly, Mary Louise. 1989. "Writing to Grow. Keeping a personal-professional journal." Heinemann. Portsmouth, New Hampshire.

Holzer, Burghild Nina. 1994. "A Walk Between Heaven & Earth: a personal journey of writing and the creative process." Three Rivers Press. 144pp.

Jetten, J. et al. 2009. "The Social Cure?" *Scientific American Mind*. September/October Issue, 2009.

Klug, Ron. 2002. "How to Keep a Spiritual Journal: a guide to journal keeping for inner growth and personal discovery."Augsburg, Minneapolis, 4th ed.

Lapworth, Katherine. 2011. "The Writer's Guide to Good Style. A Teach Yourself Book". Hodder Education. London, UK.

Moon, Jennifer. 1999. "Learning Journals: A handbook for academics, students and professional development." Kogan Page. London.

Munteanu, Nina. 2009. "The Fiction Writer: Get
Published, Write Now!" Starfire World Syndicate.
Louisville, KY. 264pp.

Munteanu, Nina. 2009. "You're Less Likely to Get Sick
if You Actively Socialize". *The Alien Next Door*:
http://sfgirl-
thealiennextdoor.blogspot.ca/2009/11/youre-less-likely-
to-get-sick-if-you.html

Munteanu, Nina. 2010. "To Facebook or Not to
Facebook: What's the Right Social Network For
You?" *The Alien Next Door.* http://sfgirl-
thealiennextdoor.blogspot.ca/2010/02/to-facebook-
or-not-to-facebook-whats.html

Munteanu, Nina. 2010. "The Writer's Toolkit". DVD set.
Starfire World Syndicate, Louisville, KY.

O'Brien, Tim. 1990. "The Things They Carried".
Houghton Mifflin. New York, NY.

Pennebaker, James. W. 1990. "Opening Up: The Healing
Power of Confiding in Others". Morrow, New York,
NY.

Pennebaker, James W., and Sandra Klihr Beall. 1986.
"Confronting a Traumatic Event: Toward an
Understanding of Inhibition and Disease." *Journal of
Abnormal Psychology* 95, no. 3: 274-81.

Plummer, Ken. 2001. "Documents of Life 2: an
invitation to a critical humanism." Sage. London.

Ross, Margaret. 2012. Counselor with Calm Waters
Counselling, New Westminster, B.C. Personal

Communication.

Schőn, Donald. 1987. "The Reflective Practitioner. How professionals think in action." Temple Smith. London.

Selfe, Cynthia. 1985. "The Electronic Pen: Computers and the Composing Process". In: Collins, James & Elizabeth A. Sommers (eds), "Writing On-line: Using Computers in the Teaching of Writing". Upper Montclair, NJ. Boynton/Cook.

Senn, Linda C. 2001. "The Many Faces of Journaling: Topics & Techniques for Personal Journal Writing". Pen Central Press. St. Louis, MO.

Ueland, Brenda. 2007. "If You Want to Write: a Book about Art, Independence and Spirit". Graywolf Press.

Vogler, Christopher. 1998. "The Writer's Journey: Mythic Structure for Writers". 2nd Edition. Michael Wiese Productions, Studio City, California. 326pp.

Wahlstrom, Ralph L. 2006. "The Tao of Writing". Adams Media. Avon, Massachusetts. 210pp.

Willliamson, Marianne. 1996. "A Return to Love: Reflections on the Principles of A Course in Miracles". Harper Paperbacks. 336pp.

Nina Munteanu is a Canadian ecologist and novelist. In addition to eight published novels, she has authored award-winning short stories, articles and non-fiction books, which have been translated into several languages throughout the world. Recognition for her work includes the *Midwest Book Review Reader's Choice Award,* finalist for *Foreword Magazine's Book of the Year Award,* the *SLF Fountain Award,* and the *Aurora Award,* Canada's top prize in science fiction.

Nina regularly publishes reviews and essays in magazines such as *The New York Review of Science Fiction* and *Strange Horizons.* She serves as staff writer for several online and print magazines, and was assistant editor-in-chief of *Imagikon,* a Romanian speculative magazine. She is currently editor of *Europa SF,* a site dedicated to serving the European SF community.

Nina lectured for over twenty years at colleges and universities, where she taught ecology, limnology & environmental education, researched and published papers in scientific journals and taught writing. Nina has been providing personal coaching and group workshops for writers on all aspects of writing and publishing in fiction and non-fiction venues for over ten years. Nina's guidebook, The Fiction Writer: Get Published, Write Now! has been adopted by schools and universities across North America and forms the basis of many of her workshops. Her award-winning blog *The Alien Next Door* hosts lively discussion on science, travel, pop culture, writing and movies. Visit www.ninamunteanu.com to find her teaching DVDs, webinars, college and university teaching engagements, and other teaching materials or to sign on for personal coaching.

Costi Gurgu is an internationally acclaimed digital artist and designer and Aurora Award finalist. He has illustrated book covers, magazine and newspaper covers and feature editorials for a variety of publications since 1999.

Costi helped design the French fashion magazine, *Madame Figaro*, and served as the art director for *Playboy* and *Tabu* magazines. He currently resides in Toronto, Canada, where he writes, teaches digital design and creates graphic designs and illustrations for various media through his company Super Pixel Design.

Anne Moody is an award-winning artist and scientist living in British Columbia, Canada. She considers herself "a realist, strongly tempted by abstract elements wrapped in story." Anne is a member of the Federation of Canadian Artists, a not-for-profit organization dedicated to the promotion and professional development of artists, and services for art collectors.

www.ingramcontent.com/pod-product-compliance
Lightning Source LLC
Chambersburg PA
CBHW021505090426
42739CB00007B/474